Fashion
Brand Stories

Fashion Brand Stories

Third edition

JOSEPH H. HANCOCK, II

BLOOMSBURY VISUAL ARTS
LONDON • NEW YORK • OXFORD • NEW DELHI • SYDNEY

BLOOMSBURY VISUAL ARTS
Bloomsbury Publishing Plc
50 Bedford Square, London, WC1B 3DP, UK
1385 Broadway, New York, NY 10018, USA
29 Earlsfort Terrace, Dublin 2, Ireland

BLOOMSBURY, BLOOMSBURY VISUAL ARTS and the Diana logo are
trademarks of Bloomsbury Publishing Plc

First edition published 2009
Second edition published 2016
This edition published 2022

A catalogue record for this book is available from the British Library.

Library of Congress Cataloging-in-Publication Data
Names: Hancock, Joseph, author.
Title: Fashion brand stories / Joseph H. Hancock, II.
Description: Third edition. | New York, NY : Bloomsbury Publishing, 2022. | Originally published
under title: Brand/story, 2009. | Includes bibliographical references and index.
Identifiers: LCCN 2022001609 | ISBN 9781350135543 (paperback) |
ISBN 9781350135567 (pdf) | ISBN 9781350135574 (epub) | ISBN 9781350135581
Subjects: LCSH: Fashion merchandising. | Advertising–Fashion. |
Branding (Marketing) | Advertising–Brand name products.
Classification: LCC HD9940.A2 H36 2022 | DDC 746.9/20688–dc23
LC record available at https://lccn.loc.gov/2022001609

ISBN: PB: 978-1-3501-3554-3
         ePDF: 978-1-3501-3556-7
        eBook: 978-1-3501-3557-4

Typeset by Integra Software Services Pvt. Ltd.
Printed and bound in India

To find out more about our authors and books visit www.bloomsbury.com
and sign up for our newsletters.

Online resources to accompany this book are available at
bloomsbury.pub/fashion-brand-stories-3e. If you experience any problems,
please contact Bloomsbury at: onlineresources@bloomsbury.com

Dedicated to:

The bravest and best mom in the world
—Peggy Miller

The most talented violinist and husband across the globe
—Raymond Mallari

The best dog
—Ruby

And to all those who have supported me over the years
—Thank you!

Contents

Preface
Brand/Story
Then and Now

Author Joseph H. Hancock, II, Ph D

Once upon a time, in 2007, I sat down with Joseph Miranda, an editor at Bloomsbury, to discuss the future of fashion branding. Fairchild Books was looking for a book with a twist that would entice students to read about the process of branding and how it influences fashion. Miranda expressed the need for an author to do a creative book, and he seemed to think I was the right person. Almost fifteen years later, it is hard to believe that I am still writing about fashion branding and storytelling, sometimes referred to as brand/story. Since the first publication of *Brand/Story: Ralph, Vera, Johnny, Bill and Other Adventures in Fashion Branding,* there have been many books written about the subject. But I have to say, Bloomsbury and I were the first. The first book sales did not take off right away, and it was almost two years later when it started to be read in classrooms. And by some of the best professors we have in our discipline, I might add!

Feedback from the first text, such as *"this book is too gay"* or *"is written like high-level journalism,"* allowed me to see success! My goal was to put diversity, equity, and inclusion into the fashion discipline, educating students about the importance of acceptance. To be honest, what's fashion without gay men or even a drag queen here or there? Or people of color and their influence in the global fashion system? And in this author's opinion, being a good scholar is not about pompous exclusion using high-level semantics, but is about inclusive words that

How To Use This Text:
Chapter Set-up

Each of the chapters in this text describes a unique concept of branding using narrative. These are case studies written in an approachable manner. The reader should then read and search out where each of these fashion companies and brands is positioned in today's marketplace. Companies do not freeze in time, and these brands have not stood still since the writing and printing of these pages. The book reveals their *brand/story*: an ideology developed in the first edition and that has carried forward.

But most importantly, this book allows us to understand each company as a *cultural entity* with its personalities and behaviors. The book is not a text of numerical analysis, but readers are encouraged to engage in the financials of each company if they choose to do so.

In each chapter are short interviews with fashion experts. These short personal brand/stories are for you to see other perspectives on the world of fashion, retail, and branding. At the end of each chapter, there are also discussion questions, exercises designed to expand your knowledge, and finally a little further exploration.

If you read this book and you go to the access points (APS), web, blogs, Facebook, Twitter, Instagram, TikTok, and other digital formats that each company has, I applaud you. This book is for stirring your curiosity about each brand. The goal is to search for company names to see what has happened since the printing of these pages. I am sure you will be surprised as you formulate your own brand/story for each company and understand how it got started. Each of these brands continues to grow and reposition itself for change. Remember, it is the people who make or break brands, whether they are consumers, merchandisers, fashion designers, store operations managers, salespeople, or even the maintenance staff at a company—and everyone must be necessary for brands to be successful. Check to see how people influence some of these brands through customer reviews, photos, and social media platforms.

I hope this book inspires you to become fascinated with both the visual spectacle and the written dialect of fashion branding that are out there to entice you to purchase products. As I tell my students, learn not to be a consuming victim, but an analytical shopper, the person who scrutinizes and understands what brands are trying to do. Share that knowledge with family and friends, but most importantly, enjoy!

Acknowledgments

This book would not have existed without the support of many individuals who helped to make it possible. First, I would like to thank Georgia Kennedy, Publisher, Fashion & Textiles Bloomsbury Visual Arts; Faith Marsland, Senior Development Editor, Fashion & Textiles, Bloomsbury Visual Arts; and the rest of the Bloomsbury team. I want to thank my family especially my mom Peggy Miller (the bravest woman in the world), my husband Raymond Mallari, and our dog Ruby. And my extended Mallari family including Rudy, Diana, Adrian, Shu, Chris, Cloud, Pork Chop, and Pumbaa. I would like to acknowledge Drexel University, Antoinette Westphal College of Media Arts & Design, the Pennoni Honors College, Women & Gender Studies, Design & Merchandising and the online Master of Science in Retail & Merchandising for all their support. To my lifelong mentor and academic mom, Patricia Cunningham, and my two academic sisters Joy Sperling and Jessica Strübel, you three mean the world to me. Thank you so much to my extraordinary friends and colleagues who suffered through the interviews in this book. I would also like to thank all the people whom Bloomsbury enlisted to review the third edition and who suggested changes. Finally, I would like to say *thank you* to everyone I have ever worked within the retailing and fashion industries as well as those in academie—you continually influence my views on fashion branding and inspire me to continue my work.

Chapter 1
Once Upon a Time: Brand/Story

Chapter Objectives

> Define fad, fashion, classic, and style
> Define fashion branding
> Give an overview of brand licensing
> Discuss the history and foundations of brand/story

Figure 1.0 French Designer, businessman and Fine Arts Academy member Pierre Cardin, 90, presents a specimen of his fragrance "Cardin by Pierre-Cardin" as he poses in his office. This fragrance was the second most-sold in the world when placed on the market in 1972. (Photo by MEHDI FEDOUACH/AFP/Getty Images)

We are what we buy, so fashion is a way to express an identity for some of us. But how do we choose one brand to purchase over the others? What makes some brands more memorable than others? The communication between a particular clothing brand and the consumer is a special connection. The retailer, manufacturer, or designer label reaches out and grabs an individual's interest through some method.

I respond to these methods when buying a new product, especially one of my favorite accessories, Coach backpacks. I have grown attached to Coach, specifically because of their current branding, along with the design of their backpacks and the methods used to merchandise them. My most recent backpack purchase was a new Hitch backpack in Black Copper/Red Sand from their Spring 2021 Collection. But what made me want to pay $695 for this bag? Through their design concepts, Coach (founded in 1941 in Manhattan) reinforces a strong sense of American historicism by selling products entrenched in the culture, designing, manufacturing, finishing, and branding. To me, Coach is the luxury accessory company of the United States because of its roots. Most of this company's product lines use utilitarian style and tie them to popular culture icons prominent in our current fashion zeitgeist.

Coach has collaborated with Keith Haring's Estate, Disney, and even stars from RuPaul's Drag Race, such as Bob the Drag Queen (Figure 1.1). Their social media and YouTube campaigns of #CoachForever for Spring Season 2021 have done quite well. The series starring Megan Thee Stallion, Kate Moss, Cole Sprouse, Debbie Harry, Kiko Mizuhara, Rickey Thompson, Bob the Drag Queen, Hari Nef, Jeremy Lin, Lexi Boling, Binx Walton, Kaia Gerber, Jon Batiste, Kelsey Lu, Paloma Elsesser, and Xiao Wen Ju is terrific to watch. By using such established celebrities (Debbie Harry, Kate Moss) and new social media personalities, Coach takes the brand from a nostalgic historical narrative to a future story about the brand. This new brand/story allows multiple meanings and a diversified array of customers to appreciate the brand. From college to Generation Xers, we can all appreciate Coach because we can identify with the story.

My memories of the brand go way back to 1990 when I purchased my first Coach briefcase (still made in the USA way back then). Coach was founded in Manhattan and, historically, was a family-run business. The brand gained impetus and soon became known as a symbol of luxury known across the United States. The brand has grown with a distinguished history of craftsmanship that has created a reputation of exceptional quality. However, Coach is known for its affordable luxury bags. They are not deviating from the ideology of a democratized American ideal of design and manufacturing. In the United States, we are not Gucci and Louis Vuitton; we believe that everyone should be able

Figure 1.1 Bob the Drag Queen models his "Gold C" clasp Coach backpack at the Premier of RuPaul's AJ and the Queen. (Photo by Presley Ann/Getty Images)

to afford a quality product without wiping out the bank account. The company will continue to be a world leader as it becomes even more popular in the Asian markets today. Coach is now a global lifestyle brand anchored in accessories, presenting a clear and compelling expression of the Coach woman and man across all product categories.[1]

As a consumer, I understand what the brand communicates and how Coach affects me to buy its products. But what makes me want to purchase from this line is more than the ideology behind this brand; it also includes the marketing of the brand, the items themselves, the sales assistants, and the actual retail store space. It is these parts combined and more. All aspects of a brand's context work together to generate a customer's desire to purchase the goods and services of a particular retailer designer if that individual understands the communication. My relationship with Coach depends on a cultural and personal tie to the brand, perhaps because I grew up in the United States with Americana historically prominent. My internalization processes include the enjoyment of these diversified historical associations from this type of storytelling. But before we go too far, let's define some basics about fashion branding.

Fashion and Popular Culture: Interview with Jessica Strübel

Dr. Jessica Strübel works at the University of Rhode Island in Textiles, Fashion Merchandising and Design, where she teaches research methods and courses on the social psychology of dress and appearance. Her research interests stem from her collective interest in anthropology and psychology. She is particularly interested in the psychological processes that culminate in realizing appearance behavior needs and understanding how material culture acquires value and meaning. Her primary research area in psychology is body image and appearance management, social media usage, and subsequent comorbid psychopathologies. In cultural studies, Jessica examines British and American popular culture as a means for fashion and cultural diffusion. She primarily explores deviant subcultures and youth cultures (e.g., music subcultures) as socialization mechanisms and resistance to class and social structure.

Where do you see new fashion brands borrowing from popular culture to sell their products?

Brands borrow from everywhere! They borrow everything from film and music to contemporary art and street style. Around you turn right now, you see corsets and Netflix's *Bridgerton*-inspired flowy, colorful, floral fashions.

Do you think most fashion brands are influenced by popular culture?

Absolutely. Designers and brands constantly observe the social surroundings and current conditions for helpful information on trend movement and directions of change. Any social shift in society is bound to influence mainstream fashion. TikTok is unavoidable (at the time of writing). More and more people are using it as a mode of self-expression, and fashion influencers are taking advantage of the platform. Designers are sharing their latest designs on TikTok, and models are even being scouted on the platform.

Even the COVID-19 pandemic has shifted face masks and comfortable casualwear into quintessential fashion items. If you look at current apparel trends, you will see that outdoor/outerwear brands, such as L.L. Bean and Patagonia, are doing quite well because people recognized the benefits of being outdoors during the pandemic. Of recent, spending time outside has often been the only physical activity some people have experienced in the past year.

Your work focuses on historically marginalized groups. Have you seen where fashion brands borrow from subcultural groups and make it mainstream fashion?

I've seen this a lot, especially with subcultures viewed as rebellious and rejecting social conventionalism. For decades the fashion industry has used subcultural styles as inspiration for mainstream apparel designs. The borrowing of styles was caused by the shift in economic importance from production to consumption. For example, since the 1970s, punk has materialized on the runways in its various iterations.

Designers frequently look to subcultures when they want to create new and shocking looks that can be mass-produced and diffused into the mass population. The neatly pre-packaged replicas reach the general public already rich in subcultural significance and meaning. As time passes and the product is consumed, the original intentions and the subcultural value are removed from the style. Industry appropriation subverts subcultural style to a mere "marketing device" for younger and younger consumers for whom the styles have no meaning. A subcultural clothing style may no longer be worn for its underlying message but simply worn for its look. This results in the unwilling emergence of subcultural groups as fashion leaders when their styles diffuse into the mass population. They are then forced to search for new forms of rebellion and expression and more subtle symbols for group differentiation. Sarah Thornton describes this as converting subcultural capital into economic capital, which threatens the subcultural dress's significance and authenticity.

Where do you see the future of fashion branding as it relates to popular culture?

I see it continuing to borrow from those people who are regarded as innovators. Mass production and consumption have allowed subcultural styles to become the norm. The consumption of commodities, such as clothing and music, is central to the construction and declaration of one's identity, especially for youth who find themselves in a constant flux of invention and reinvention of their identities. However, we could argue that the instability in one's identity results in a lack of substance. Identity is now managed by the series of styles through which an individual adopts. Post-subculturalists do not have to worry about rules, ideological commitment, or even the contradictions between their identities, which are "forged by appearance." Identity has become something to try on (like clothing), use temporarily, and then dispose of for a newer, more fashionable one.

What Is Fashion Versus Style?

Many readers may already know how to define *fashion*, but those who may not be devotees of the subject should know what it is and how it is defined. There are various types of dress, and to understand how the fashion industry works, one must understand the differences between a *fad*, a *classic*, *fashion*, and *style*.

A *fad* is an item that becomes popular for a moment in time but then vanishes quickly, to return later or never again. A great example of an older fad that disappeared never to return is the Sony Walkman, which became popular in the 1980s because it enabled a person to play audio cassette tapes and the radio while walking around or even exercising. Today's version is a mobile device player such as an iPod. I do not think we will ever see the rebirth of the Sony Walkman audio cassette player. Another example was Nike-produced *Livestrong* Lance Armstrong yellow rubber wristbands that everyone was wearing for the Lance Armstrong Livestrong Cancer Foundation. While Armstrong was in the media's good graces, Nike fans wore the yellow wristbands, but they soon vanished after the public discovered that Armstrong was accused of doping to win his cycling races.

A *classic* is a particular or distinctive garment that never goes out of style. Examples are T-shirts, baseball caps, blue jeans, and Oxford cloth shirts. Although classics never go out of style, their design or style might change. For example, blue jean styles change over time; however, the actual garment "blue jean" is the same. Recent years have had everyone wearing skinny jeans, but everyone wore bellbottoms during some periods (remember Jnco jeans?). Both garments are forms of the classic blue jean, even though the silhouette, style, and design change. Even T-shirts have various silhouettes and have gone from trim fitting to regular fit. Screen printing makes T-shirts appear trendy, but they are still classic.

Fashion is the prevailing style at a particular time. Remember skinny jeans? They have recently been what we would call *in fashion*, but we probably move in a new direction to fuller-fitting jeans. Blue jean fashions change. One season the style can be dark and unwashed, and in the next season, it can be tattered and torn with the jean washed out. A fashion can be what the latest magazine dictates that everyone has to buy for the new season; if that garment becomes widespread, it becomes fashion. The world is a large place, and many fashions are happening simultaneously. What we wear in the Northern Hemisphere as fashion is different from what we wear in the Southern Hemisphere. Most importantly, it is not what is worn but how it is branded that makes it fashionable.

Now, *style* is another area as well. If we refer back to the photo of Bob the Drag Queen (Figure 1.1). What Bob is wearing forms personal style and appearance expressions of himself. Style is how we put various apparel and garments together to create a look. Style does not have to be in fashion; however, your style can be fashionable. Styles can be unique or in sync with the zeitgeist and what everyone is wearing. Most of us like to have a style that fits everyone, so we do not stand out. However, someone like Vivienne Westwood believes that her style should stand out, and she has made that sort of expression a form of fashion (see Chapter 4). Whatever the case, style can be or could have been fashion, but it does not necessarily reflect current fashion. Style is unique to an individual's personal taste and sometimes expresses their personality.

What Is Fashion Branding?

For this book and our purposes, fashion branding is "the *cumulative image* of a product or service that consumers quickly associate with a particular brand; it offers an overall experience that is unique, different, special and identifiable."[2] Branding is also "a *competitive strategy* that targets customers with products, advertising, and promotion organized around a coherent message as a way to encourage the purchase and repurchase of products from the same company."[3] Branding is not just about individual products; it also creates an identity for the company. This volume focuses on creating a perception generated through *brand storytelling*, or what I refer to as *brand/story*.

Fashion branding is the context that surrounds the garment and the image that designers, retailers, manufacturers, and promotional consultants create to encourage consumers to buy new items. Fashion branding can make fashion seem fun, exciting, innovative, and unique; fashion brands need a solid identity to be understood by consumers. Fashion branding shapes and contextualizes a garment or accessory to establish its identity.

A T-shirt, pair of jeans, skirt, sweater, pair of khaki pants, baseball cap, and even a pair of shoes can be dull and indistinguishable from others without the help of fashion branding. Whereas couture garments rely on craftsmanship to sell, mass-produced products depend on branding to make them appear unique among their competitors. But branding has allowed luxury brands to gain more considerable appeal and become global fashion commodities sold even among mass-market consumers.

An excellent historical example of this is Pierre Cardin (Figure 1.0), the master of branding, licensing, and global sales. He was the first to take a luxury name and license it to sell mass-produced products that sometimes reflected a lower quality. In 1959, Cardin was the first designer to show ready-to-wear garments on the fashion runway at the department store Printemps in Paris. In other words, he is the man responsible for taking clothes people wore and making them runway fashion. Historically, a fashion show was only for the most exclusive customer. Cardin democratized it and included garments that were affordable and obtainable to a larger audience. He established himself as a luxury brand with an immediate internationally recognizable reputation.

His ability to "rent" his name to other companies, or what is mainly referred to as *licensing*, gave him an enormous reputation in fashion. This designer's status and unique logo appeared on everything from fragrance, timepieces, neckties, and sunglasses to even food and furniture! Because Pierre Cardin's name was associated with high-quality luxury style, the company was able to license across many consumer product categories giving him a global presence in Japan, China, and Russia (before the age of the computer). His fashion shows in China were the first European fashion designs to grace their runways. He paved the way for others to enter the Asian market. And even today, his fragrance Pierre Cardin (the same bottle he is holding in Figure 1.0) is one of the most noted in this category, all done by branding.

Fashion branding is the process whereby designers, manufacturers, strategists, creative directors, retailers, and those responsible for selling fashion create campaigns and give fashion garments a unique identity. As stated before, branding is not just about the product; branding is also about creating a clear vision and strategy for a company. Branding gives everyone involved a clear direction and focus.

Although many people have written about brands, few have examined fashion brands and looked at those who sell fashion brands as storytellers. This book aims to describe what goes into a fashion brand and show how each featured company has developed a unique *brand/story* for itself and its products.

A Short Brand/Story   **Public Relations Branding: Interview with Anne Peirson-Smith**

Former public relations (PR) expert turned professor, and Course Leader, MA International Fashion Management at Nottingham Trent University, Dr. Anne Peirson-Smith discusses the real side of PR and its importance for effective fashion business management. Her book, *Public Relations in Asia Pacific: Communicating Across Cultures*, contains various articles on the topic of PR, validating her expertise as a PR guru, and is the complete guide to understanding the world of PR in different types of consumer markets and cultural contexts.

Can you tell us a little about yourself and your background as a professor and public relations executive?

I always find myself wearing two "hats" in my life—as the PR professional and the professor. I entered the public relations and branding industries over twenty years ago while I was doing research for my PhD at Sheffield University in the UK. As a student, I had previously completed an undergraduate course in History at

(Continued)

St. Andrews University and had a Master's in Communication and Information Studies at Sheffield University in the UK, in addition to a professional law qualification. Essentially, I found that the PR profession used all of the knowledge and analytical skills that I had acquired during my studies and satisfied an enquiring mind. So, I started out working with the Saatchi group in London handling clients such as Apple and then moved to Hong Kong with US PR agency Burson Marsteller. In this capacity, I worked for a range of multinational clients across various PR accounts from Johnson & Johnson and French Connection to M&S and Armani. In doing so, I experienced a cross section of invaluable PR roles in public affairs, consumer relations, marketing communications, branding, corporate training, and crisis management. This wide-ranging portfolio of strategic professional experience illustrates the increasingly inclusive nature of PR as a one-stop communications shop.

It was clear from my entry point into the PR profession twenty years ago that this was a fast-growing creative industry that was starting to gain recognition in the UK and Asia as a corporate and branding communications necessity, given the increasing need to manage image and reputation among a company's stakeholders across mediated channels and in particular with the take-up of social media engagement by fashion brands at all levels of the marketplace. Also, PR always had the potential to be a one-stop shop as communications efforts started to integrate rapidly throughout the past decade with increased digitization and technological advancements and the heightened dominance of social media. It was also important to recognize that PR was not about spin or just about press relations but adapted to the dynamic corporate climate and integrated a range of communication management functions including public, government, community, marketing, corporate, consumer, and financial affairs – all in the name of establishing a positive position for the brand in the mindset of stakeholders.

When I was working in the PR and branding industry in Hong Kong, one of my many PR roles was as a corporate trainer in media skills and crisis response management for various international clients, and it reminded me how much I missed teaching and research in the academy. So, I returned to academic life, taking up a professorship at Hong Kong Baptist University School of Communication teaching Media Studies, PR, and Advertising and moving more recently to City University of Hong Kong to run the Professional and Creative Communication undergraduate program. This was a timely move, as globally higher educational institutions were realizing the importance of establishing industry connections as a critical career through-train for students.

While I have kept active and updated in the field engaging in PR consultancy work for Executive Counsel Ltd., a medium-sized Hong Kong-based PR and public affairs firm, I also teach, research, and write about the subject of PR, given its rising importance in the communications and creative industries, the need for people to understand it more, and why a fashion organization at any market level, for example, needs to manage identity, reputation, and image to survive and thrive as a competitive company in differentiating itself from the competition and developing support from investors, partners, and employees. In addition, I assist my students in getting placements in PR, marketing, and branding companies to enable them to experience the realities of the workplace outside of the classroom. There is no substitute for real work experience.

Effective PR practice enables a brand to develop strong, enduring relationships across key stakeholder groups built on trust to protect its reputational status and ultimately the bottom line with return on investment (ROI) being measured in terms of traditional impact on sales and more recently in a digital world, cost per clicks, and cost per engagement impacting on brand awareness. Interestingly, PR people are the invisible hand behind media releases, social media posts, blogs, and CEO speeches, and it should be kept that way, as a successful form of communications management should appear to be a natural way of highlighting a company's existence and achievements in the eyes of its many stakeholders, from customers to competitors.

Fashion is a global industry with multinational dimensions, and it is also important to understand the cultural nuances of fashion branding as markets rapidly emerge across China and Asia complete with their own brands. Critically, we need to realize that one size does not fit all in communicating a brand globally as local cultural accommodations are needed to adapt to each market situation. As I noted in a previous book on the topic of managing PR across Asia Pacific, the value systems are different in the more collectivist, high-context cultures of Asia, which will affect the content of promotional appeals and messages. When launching in China 2005, Fendi used the Great Wall as a giant catwalk, generating significant local and global attention in the process of localizing their global presence and highlighting their unique differential.

Why do you think a good fashion brand image is important to have in the eyes of the public?

"I don't design clothes, I design dreams." Ralph Lauren.

It is now critical for a fashion brand to have a clearly defined identity and positive image in the consumer imagination in order to differentiate itself from the competition and enable the consumer to understand its real importance in their lives through the promise that it makes to deliver core values—whether that's quality, value for money, exclusivity, heritage, or sustainability. This is particularly important in the fashion and lifestyle sectors, whether we are talking about a value brand such as Uniqlo or a luxury brand such as Hermès, in addition to the sustainable initiatives of H&M or GAP. The brand image is based on customer perceptions and is open to influence in terms of how the brand communicates its story and creates a brand experience. A company's brand is akin to a person's reputation, and it has to be earned. Public relations and its ability to manage reputation are a critical component in this brand management process and is increasingly given credit as a management process for breathing life into the fashion brand based on symbolic capital, beyond the tangible aspects of the name and logo. It's all about doing good things—having a great product, contributing to environmental protection or engaging with a community outreach program, and getting public credit for this, while generating third-party endorsements from fashion influencers, bloggers, and tweeters to journalists across a range of communications and social media channels. Planned, strategic, omni-channel communication is now needed for every fashion brand to develop strong stakeholder relationships and engender a favorable understanding between the fashion brand and its publics to position it securely in the marketplace. By way of illustration, a fashion brand marketing a pair of jeans must persuade consumers that this is the only pair of jeans for them in terms of "coolness" or artisanal "heritage," inclusivity, or sustainable sourcing and production, which is all strategically managed through engaging brand storytelling across omni-channel media platforms.

Strategic PR campaigns run by value fashion brands such as H&M or Zara, for example, or luxury brands such as Burberry or Louis Vuitton, aim to capture consumer attention and develop key relationships or long-lasting communities by positioning and sustaining their presence and profile across multiple communication platforms, from offline print media to online social media, by creating and managing brand identity and image through expert storytelling using influencers, for example. These brand communities are driven by shared interest and values generating positive conversations that impact on ROI representing a bundle of soft metrics: brand visibility, realization, and positivity. Remember, fashion PR is not just about the garments you sell, but the stories that you tell about them!

Also, as fashion brands, like all organizations, are now more accountable given the more open access to communication channels by netizens, it is more important than ever to manage communication proactively and be in control of brand messaging. Of course, issues such as sustainability and inclusivity need to be managed in an ongoing way by fashion brands, ensuring that the right values are being represented in practice such as the use of fair-trade labor or ethical textile sourcing practices. Additionally, crises confront all organizations on a regular basis and fashion brands are not immune to that. Taking a proactive approach to brand management is a critical survival strategy for fashion brands who must always be prepared for the next crisis and have a crisis communication plan in place to manage the media and consumer responses in case a fashion brand is found to be behaving unethically by dumping excess inventory into landfill or being culturally insensitive, as D&G have sometimes found.

Public relations offers the perfect communications toolkit to communicate brand identity and manage corporate image across a host of multiple channels from print to digital. It is premised on what messages we offer to customers, especially in terms of projecting brand personality when crafting the emotional brand–consumer connections through skillful visual and verbal narratives embedded in strategically crafted key messages. This integrated promotional effort is orchestrated by the PR professional across multiple platforms in the process of forging and maintaining valuable stakeholder relationships to endorse the brand as a way of providing credibility and establishing trust aligned with consumer and stakeholder values.

Essentially, in terms of brand storytelling, a fashion brand should stay true to the brand promise when creating and managing a relatable brand personality for the brand follower. It should also actively engage the audience in its story regarding visual content and involvement through social media-driven engagement by getting the consumer to tell and extend your brand story as a form of co-creation. The aim is to convert customers into brand champions and fashion fans who love their brand even more than they love its products. Think of the "Customize Your Converse" campaign, TOMS Shoes' "The Bid for Better" digital initiative, or Burberry's "The Art of the Trench."

Do you think that fashion brands need to have a strong sense of style?

There is no doubt that fashion brands do need a distinctive sense of style as part of their brand identity. One of the foundations of good branding is memorability, and this should be expressed through the brand identity and be encapsulated in its style. Ideally, this should be conveyed through the physical attributes of the logo and product, in addition to the symbolic intangibles of the brand's personality and presence. Also, brand uniqueness should be narrated compellingly in the brand storytelling process across all of the promotional collaterals that the brand produces, right through to point of sale and attention-grabbing window displays and on social media platforms such as Instagram or Weibo. It should be embedded in what the brand is in terms of its visual identity—logos, packaging, collections—and how it behaves and expresses its personality in store or online via blogs and social media. This style identity should be instantly recognizable—think of the ubiquitous look and feel of the Ralph Lauren stores globally, the East–West

(Continued)

aesthetic of Shanghai Tang, or the Boho chic edgy-ness of Planet Blue or Threadsence. As Coco Chanel wisely advised, "In order to be irreplaceable, one must always stand out."

Do you think a company's style and ability to follow fashion are the same?

"Fashion fades. Style is eternal." Yves Saint Laurent

Fashion and style are two different but interrelated things. As I see it, fashion is about the look and image that are popular in a specific period of time—for example, the 1960s or the 2000s. Alternatively, style is more about expressing individuality and uniqueness through clothes, and is invested with timeless quality, without an expiration date. So, fashion is the resource providing the inspiration and style is what you do with it.

Of course, fashion brands from Chanel to Cos pay attention to trend forecasting and what is happening on the streets as a source of creative inspirations for its design teams. But a brand should be leading the trends as opposed to following them to be an iconic brand. The PR mindset is about proactive planning and supports a trend forecasting approach to brand management.

Also, fashion brands should certainly have a defined style—think of iconic streetwear brands such as A Bathing Ape or Supreme. Brand equity relies on defining fashion trends and not following them slavishly as a way of being at the front of the consumer mindset, unless it wants to be a forgettable brand that is soon discarded and relegated to the remainder bins. Whether you agree with Giorgio Armani in considering that "The difference between style and fashion is quality," or Ralph Lauren, "Fashion is over quickly. Style is forever," there is no doubt that brands should pay attention to curating fashion collections with a focus on a distinctive style, enabling consumers to express their individuality, yet at the same time being mindful of sustaining their presence.

In the future, do you think fashion branding is going to become more or less significant in this industry?

Over a decade ago, veteran fashion journalist Terri Agins predicted the end of fashion as we know it with haute couture being overtaken by name-brand mass marketing, where hype was more important than the product on offer. More recently, veteran stylist Li Edelkoort has warned of the same fate for fashion, citing wider reasons, including an elitist, misguided fashion education system falsely preparing young designers for celebrity success, unethical sweatshop production, and blogger-driven advertorial commercial content for the "like" generation. Yet, while these are valid concerns, the role of fashion branding is more needed than ever to address these challenges facing the fashion system in a post-COVID-19 future to keep brands on track and relevant for their consumers by implementing sustainable production and consumption practices across the global supply chain and keeping an active and visible digital presence.

If they are to survive, then fashion brands at all levels, from high end to high street, will need to rework and re-evaluate their brand strategies and marketing efforts using a proactive PR approach to attract younger customers from the upcoming generations, while at the same time retaining their existing loyal fan followers. Hence, we see luxury brands such as Dior, Gucci, Balenciaga, Chanel, or Versace globally reinventing their image for a younger generation of luxury shoppers by developing digital content, generating more social media presence, and hiring younger designers to create new activewear-inspired product lines.

Niche online apparel retailers, such as ASOS and Farfetch, are fast emerging on the fashion branding landscape and relocating the directional power with the consumer using crowdfunding business models whereby items are only produced if they generate enough backers.

New companies appearing across the global fashion system mean that multiple communication channels, increasingly digital and mobile, will be used to maintain active relationships with different generations of followers. Put simply, a carefully crafted PR brand strategy for brands of all shapes and sizes with value-driven content strongly aligned with consumer and stakeholder interests will enable a brand to manage this juggling act and remain relevant in order to survive and thrive in the longer term.

How difficult is it to have a career in public relations?

Public relations has certainly come of age and in many ways it is the communications industry of the moment. Its time has come due to the need for all companies to activate good multi-way, omni-channel communication with interested parties representing a good career opportunity. Brand guru Al Ries predicted the rise of PR and the fall of advertising nearly twenty years ago, and this visionary viewpoint was not far off.

In order to work in the industry, a degree in communications is not a fixed requirement. The profession is open to anyone who has good people skills, is a good written and spoken communicator, is able to multitask, can work under pressure, has no ego (as you will not see your name or byline in lights!), is able to generate creative solutions to client challenges, and has a positive, can-do attitude at all times.

Gaining as much PR experience as possible is crucial in terms of determining what you want to do and what you prefer to do, as the industry has so many options, from agency work for the large multinationals, such as

Burson Marsteller, Ketchum Newscan, and Ogilvy, or smaller specialist fashion PR agencies, such as Style House PR or Elle Communications, in addition to working in-house for fashion brands themselves. Jobs in fashion PR can also take two forms – corporate PR, managing the company's identity and image as part of the core communications team or product/marketing PR, involving promoting a fashion product, line, or brand.

Internships are the best way to get to know the PR industry in an early career stage to get an insight into how PR works and also to build upon an important work portfolio of clients. As fashion PR and PR in general are a competitive industry at entry point, it is important to work on your own personal brand to differentiate yourself from the crowd of other applicants. Hence, having a blog and compiling an eye-catching portfolio of PR experience with a passion for, and knowledge of, the fashion industry are crucial. Finally, be a consummate connector! It's necessary to develop skills as a networker by attending PR events, fashion events, and events organized by professional associations, as this may help gain entry into a job via a key industry contact or professional network and also will help in developing career progression once you are working inside the industry.

When you represent a fashion company or celebrity, do you think that it's important for you to look a certain way? Do you have to "brand" Anne?

In both the communication and fashion industries, it is important to present yourself well and in a differentiated way—to walk the talk as it were and to use this powerful form of visual communication to engender trust and confidence from the client or company that you represent. Again, it's back to locating a recognizable, yet unique look and feel for the brand or person and expressing it consistently across all communication channels. On a personal level, brand "me" is still a work in progress and takes multiple forms depending on the context in which I'm operating—as we all perform many roles, I wear at least two hats in my professional life as academic and PR consultant. The rule of thumb for me is always to express my personal style in terms of the presentation of self and in the outputs that I produce and publish to differentiate myself and add to the knowledge base of the fashion business. Yet, as the fashion industry increasingly faces a range of enhanced social and issues-based challenges across its supply and value chains in a post-COVID-19 world from sustainability and inclusivity to technologization, we should remember that clothes aren't going to save the world, but the people who make, manage, and wear them might well do so.

Fashion Branding and Storytelling

In their book, *Storytelling: Branding in Practice*, Klaus Fog, Christian Budtz, and Baris Yakaboylu describe storytelling as the means for creating a brand. The storytelling process relies on a company's ability to make an emotional connection through its brand and to build target markets.[4] Fog et al. believe that a brand reaches full consumption potential when it makes an emotional connection with consumers, when its consumers and employees can understand its values and messages. Storytelling is the vehicle that communicates these values in a process that is easy for consumers to understand. Storytelling speaks to the emotions of the target market, which in return becomes loyal to the company.[5]

Fog et al. describe how advertising reflects the basic concepts of storytelling, which they define as message, conflict, character, and plot. Advertising uses the same formula and can pique consumer interest while building associations with certain products and creating emotional meaning.[6] For example, Apple has continually recreated its brand through creative marketing. It seems that the fundamental basis for its branding concept is to create social and political communities.[7] Products such as the iPad with all its functions and applications allow the company to demonstrate how its products appeal to a multitude of individuals from all walks of life. Apple still sells its iPod nano and iPod shuffle (PRODUCT) RED special edition, donating all the profits of these items to fight AIDS in Africa. (PRODUCT) RED, created by the musician Bono and his colleague Bobby Shriver, allows Apple to make a political statement supporting AIDS awareness—Go Apple!

Apple's personification of its brand was done in the "Are You a Mac or PC?" campaign (2007) featuring two individuals: one who pretends to be a Mac computer and the other who pretends to be a PC. Each individual tells a story about who he is and how he performs. The character's appearance is crucial. Representing the PC is a nerdy, overweight, suit-wearing executive type, whereas a trim, young, and attractive jean- and sneaker-wearing, hip, young man defines the Apple Mac computer. The PC seems uptight and inefficient, whereas the Apple is relaxed and very efficient, thus building a social community in which "Apple people" are sexy, attractive, calm, casual, and successful. Who would you want to be?

If you are skeptical of the whole idea of storytelling and the importance of branding as a means of building a company's name and appearance for mass consumption, then think about Coca-Cola. This company reaches a global market and has created an iconic image with its red-and-white label that people know worldwide. But did you know that Coca-Cola is responsible for creating the familiar Santa Claus in the red-and-white suit (Figure 1.2)? In 1931 Coca-Cola introduced the character and included him over the years in various poses, with elves. In different scenarios, it generated stories about Santa and co-branded him (Santa with Coca-Cola) and at the same time personified its product. People began associating Santa with Coca-Cola, and now each year, the company comes out with commemorative cans and bottles of its product with Santa Claus's image printed on them. How's that for a great brand/story?

Coca-Cola is not the only brand that believes characters are best for selling. Many companies like to personify or create a specific character for their brands so that people relate to them better. Personification

Figure 1.2 An advertisement in 1953 shows a young boy in pink pajamas watching Santa Claus as he takes a Coca-Cola from the refrigerator. Created by Haddon Sundblom. (Photo by Library of Congress/Corbis/VCG via Getty Images)

SERVE Coca-Cola

REFRESHING SURPRISE

assigns personal and human characteristics to a brand or item that is nonhuman. Mr. Clean gives a household cleaner emotional appeal; Flo from Progressive Insurance makes insurance exciting because she brings it to life, and Mickey and Minnie Mouse are constantly promoting Disney World.

Even the US big-box retailer Target creates an experiential process for their consumers through Bullseye, their mascot dog (Figure 1.3). Since 1999, he has become the Target Corporation symbol and generates personified excitement for the brand even in the store space. His influence is so significant customers can even take photographs with him in their stores (Figure 1.4). Bullseye has become the symbol for the second-largest retailer in the United States and across the globe that you can even shop Bullseyeshop.com and read the Target newsletter called *A Bullseye View*. Most folks know that Target's logo is the bullseye, but this dog creates another version of a living logo, so when people see Bullseye (the dog), they think Target! This is a double win for the Target Corporation with two noted identifiers for the brand.

Figure 1.3 Actor Shemar Moore and Bullseye the Target dog attend the tenth annual GLSEN Respect Awards at the Regent Beverly Wilshire Hotel on October 17, 2014 in Beverly Hills, California. (Photo by Jonathan Leibson/Getty Images for GLSEN Respect Awards, Los Angeles)

Figure 1.4 Customers can get their photos taken with Bullseye in Target's Children's Departments. (Photo by the author, all rights reserved)

The Goals of this Book

This book aims to educate, entertain, shock, and enlighten readers, building your passion for branding. To help you fully understand and apply the information, each chapter ends with discussion questions and methods for expanding your knowledge. The book stimulates the traditional inundation of heavy theoretical concepts and monumental statistical analysis; the text is approachable. It aims to enable the reader to go out into the world and experience fashion branding firsthand.

The third edition of *Fashion Brand Stories* presents a pop-cultural critical perspective. In other words, the goal is to question what each fashion brand is trying to communicate, understand why companies contextualize products the way they do, and start to think critically, not taking fashion branding for face value. Explore these existing brands and read about them in both scholarly and mass publications. *Gain your own opinion* and know the facts about each company's brand/story after this book has introduced them.

It is essential to think analytically and learn to *read* and *critique* the facts. You need to understand each brand's advertisements and what they are trying to tell you to clarify the company's intentions. In today's computerized world, everyone is spoon-fed information; this text encourages critical thinking. As the author, I chose to discuss certain brands based on responses from thousands of individuals that stated they liked these particular brands, and I do too! The reader needs to *think*: what do a company's biography and its advertising say about that company? How does the company's message make consumers want to buy or not buy? Are the images that are created positive or negative?

This text presents many types of fashion brands, allowing you to make your own decisions about each particular company. I give my opinions here and there, but I want you to have one too! All the fashion companies, interviewees, and editors who participated in this book's production encourage readers to visit the brands' websites, sign up for email lists, and especially visit stores. After all, the book is about adventures and explorations.

Although some texts try to quantify brands as a form of consumer behavior and empirical research to explain fashion branding scientifically, this book uses a qualitative, hermeneutical approach and meaning-based reflection to generate critical thinking. Those who wish to investigate numerical data can visit a database such as the Mintel Reports.

Moving Beyond Fashion Brand Stories

Fashion Brand Stories, Third Edition, encourages participation in popular culture. As the reader, you will need to develop your knowledge about fashion brands and their images in the media. So, it is probably a good idea to supplement this book with magazines such as *W, Vogue, GQ,* even *Men's Health*. I would also encourage using how-to-brand textbooks such as *Fashion Branding Unraveled* (Bloomsbury, 2011) by Kaled Hameide or *Brand Management Strategies* (Bloomsbury, 2016) by William D'Ariesnzo. They both describe the various branding components in easy-to-understand terms.

When you read the chapters, refer to company websites, business periodicals, and other magazines to see what has recently happened at a particular company since the writing of this book. You need to look at as many publications as possible in addition to the internet; after all, it is in print where fashion branding presents as artwork in texture and form and where the average consumer still views it.

Although some of the book's brands could be considered a little controversial, I offer no apology. In a fashion merchandising, design, and strategy world, there has been one tried-and-true motto: *think outside the box* and leave your comfort zone! I have also chosen to use companies whose branding represents diversity because the fashion industry is one of the most assorted casts of characters you will ever meet. I have decided to use companies whose branding methods are innovative, who have made significant contributions. To keep consumers interested, many brands relate to various types of people, and so do authors. I expose you to a diverse array of fashion brands representing the fashion industry to show how new products reach us globally. For those interested in a bit of history, there is some information in this text you will enjoy as well! Happy reading.

Discussion Questions

1. What is fashion branding? How does branding establish a product's identity? Give five good examples.
2. How can companies sell items such as T-shirts, jeans, and sunglasses at high prices? Can you give an example of another item sold in the luxury market that might not be perceived as a luxury good?
3. Race, ethnicity, religion, sexual orientation, gender, and age play a part in purchasing decisions. Identify three consumer groups that are different from you. In your opinion, how do they differ from each other concerning fashion and the types of brands they purchase?

Expand Your Knowledge

Find a fashion ad to share with your class. Identify any historical, social, political, or pop culture icons in the ad and share the story the ad might be trying to convey to the viewer. Back up your analytical discussion with facts found from academic sources such as art, literature, history, and business. Who are the target markets of this ad? Why? How does this ad make the consumer want to purchase the product?

Further Exploration

Watch:
Naomi Klein, *No Logo: Brands, Globalization, Resistance* (Iron Weed Films, 2009), https://www.youtube.com/watch?v=oeTgLKNb5R0 (accessed December 17, 2021).
Read:
Kaled K. Hameide, *Fashion Branding Unraveled* (New York: Fairchild Books, 2011).
Mark Tungate, *Fashion Brands: Branding Style from Armani to Zara* (Philadelphia: Kogan Page, 2012).

I dreamed

I stood

the shou...

in my

maidenform

bra

...ETTE*... **best-loved Maidenform bra**... now in care-free, iron-free Dacron†. Famous, fabulous combination ...d spoke-stitched cups for superb fit, luscious curves. White, iced champagne, black. A, B, C cups, 2.50. D cup, 3...

†White Broadcloth: Cotton, "Dacron" Poly...

Chapter 2
The Past, Present, and Future: A Conceptual Overview

Chapter Objectives

> Discuss the history of fashion branding
> Examine historical postmodern theories of fashion and their conceptual implications with branding
> Describe the shift from postmodernism to hypermodernism
> Discuss contemporary marketing and consumer theories and their essential applications to fashion branding
> Ignite conversation about the impact of shifting consumer demographics and implications for the future of fashion brands

Figure 2.0 Maidenform Bra Advertisement, 1962. (Courtesy of Advertising Archives)

There is usually a theoretical or academic side to understanding each text, and this chapter is it. For readers, these chapters usually do not awaken excitement for learning and understanding because they are full of heavy jargon and unapproachable interpretations of theory (trust, this author has been there). But there is hope that you will enjoy learning about critical theory, hermeneutics, and conceptual ideas of fashion branding with this text.

Fashion branding became necessary as the popularity of mass fashion grew in the twentieth century. Developments in clothing production and media allowed fashion to diffuse through society rapidly. The growing acceptance of ready-to-wear clothes and sportswear, as well as advances in manufacturing technologies, led to the quick design and distribution of garments at all social-class levels. The theory of simultaneous adoption of fashion suggests that clothes enter at all consumer market levels with variations in quality and price line to accommodate consumer spending power. This variation allows each consumer to follow a current style according to his or her interests and budget. Manufacturers and retailers have catered to the middle- and lower-end markets by designing and producing garments for these more price-conscious consumers.[1]

For their garments to achieve prominence, retailers and manufacturers had to adopt various promotion methods to target specific types of clientele. Mass marketing included fashion branding directed at all consumer groups. Brands such as Bradley, Voorhees & Day, commonly known as BVD (Figure 2.1), exemplified the "everyman" quality of advertising common in the first half of the twentieth century.

During the late nineteenth and early twentieth centuries (c. 1890–1945), fashion emphasized the value of function and use. Consumers were influenced by the practicality, style, fabrication, and availability of new products.[2] It is important to remember that many clothing items were *new* to consumers, and they had perhaps never seen mass-manufactured things before. Advertisements focused on giving consumers the features (fabric, fit, color, style) and benefits (functionality—durability, warmth) that were important to them.

These same ideas are present in other fashion-related industries such as beauty. The early twentieth-century cosmetics giant Madame C.J. Walker, the first self-made female millionaire, philanthropist, and activist in the United States, was the Oprah of her time. Mrs. Charles James (C.J.) Walker is known for her health and beauty toiletries sold through her salons, street markets, and door-to-door. She created advertisements that were both informative and inspiring for women to see the company's entire line of products (Figure 2.2). The copy reads, "If you want beauty of complexion and loveliness of hair, try Mme C.J. Walker's renowned

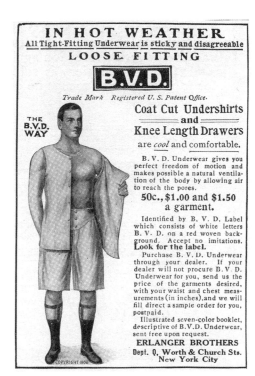

Figure 2.1 Advertisement for BVD underwear by Erlanger Brothers in New York, 1907. (Photo by Jay Paull/Getty Images)

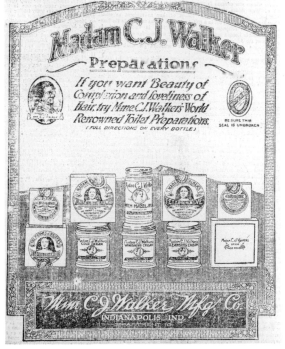

Figure 2.2 An advertisement for cosmetic products by Madame C.J. Walker, New York, 1920. (Photo by Library of Congress)

Figure 2.3 Portrait of Madame C.J. Walker (born Sarah Breedlove, 1867–1919), 1913. (Photo by Addison N. Scurlock)

toilet preparations." Walker (Figure 2.3) specialized in Black hair care, which was previously ignored in the mass market. Her brand set up schools and trained young women to sell door-to-door and perform spa-like services. She was the first of her kind and an inspiration to future beauty marketers like Estée Lauder, who would borrow some of Walker's techniques.

Celebrity endorsement is prevalent during this period. This was not only an innovation of the late twentieth and early twenty-first centuries. These were the early days of television and film, and what better way to get new products introduced into the market than to have celebrities promote them? Such stars as Johnny Weissmuller and Mae West announced and inspired creations from swimwear to perfume. Weissmuller, an Olympic champion and best known for playing Tarzan in films from the 1930s through the 1940s, promoted BVD swimwear (Figure 2.4). At this time, BVD diversified its brand from underwear to swimwear to increase sales. Weissmuller's name sold millions of swimsuits and sponsorship swim camps across the country.[3]

And while you may think Marilyn Monroe or Madonna were the first blonde bombshells and prominent female activists in media, in the 1930s, it was film legend Mae West whose curves epitomized the perfect female shape. West, a leading businesswoman, produced her

Figure 2.4 January 13, 1932: Child star Jackie Cooper takes a lesson from Olympic swimming champion and Hollywood actor Johnny Weissmuller (1904–84). Weissmuller is wearing a BVD swimsuit. The company then employed him as a swimwear and underwear model. (Photo via John Kobal Foundation/ Getty Images)

Figure 2.5 Mae's mannequin c. 1933: Mae West (1893–1980) stands behind a mannequin made to her measurements. The labels read: Kate Smith, large; Mae West, perfect 36; Miriam Hopkins, boyish. (Photo via John Kobal Foundation/Getty Images)

films and took on risqué (deemed immoral) productions of drag shows in the 1930s and challenged the idea that you had to be small to be accepted. In Figure 2.5, Mae West was in a promo shoot representing the "perfect" woman's shape; Elsa Schiaparelli used West's shape for her perfume bottle for the fragrance Shocking Pink. Their connection arose when West requested that Schiaparelli design the clothing for her film *Every Day's a Holiday* (Paramount, 1937). The perfume was a smashing success and sold across the country with West as an inspiration for the product's packaging and a prominent endorser.

Both Weissmuller and Mae West demonstrate how powerful celebrity endorsements worked to build consumer trust to sell newly marketed products to the public. They also reveal that one of the effective branding strategies used today is not innovative or new but is a continuation of a tradition that is around a hundred years old.

Earlier in the twentieth century, brands such as Burberry introduced new and innovative sportswear clothing to the public. To do so, they utilized two methods of fashion branding that were common at this time. First, Burberry explained the product by emphasizing the function of golf apparel (Figure 2.6). In this image, the text reads, "Golf

Figure 2.6 Advert for Burberry sports clothes showing a man and woman playing golf, 1948. (Photo by Universal History Archive/Universal Images Group via Getty Images)

Jerkins—weatherproof gabardine or leather," demonstrating product benefits. After all, this was an innovation to encourage consumer spending. Second, Burberry illustrates how to wear the garments. This golf wear ad is a forerunner to advertising that emphasizes *context* and placement of the product as a key selling strategy. *Context* is the medium, circumstances, or situation in which the product and the message (the ad) are transmitted and received. In this Burberry example, the context is the use of a print ad (medium) and the text and illustration within the ad.

During this time, there was an explosion of products from a vast array of manufacturers and retailers using visual illustrations of context to demonstrate the features and benefits of products and how the consumer could use a garment for a specific function. Burberry took a higher stance on craftsmanship and quality, giving them a future edge in the luxury brand category.

The Burberry ad reflects ideals after the Second World War, when technology, transportation, and communications rapidly improved and mass production increased. Returning veterans began to move to the suburbs to start families. Fashion retailers, manufacturers, and designers began to strategize about how they could benefit from this social trend. The mass markets began to grow, and consumers began spending more on achieving an American dream lifestyle. The concept of "keeping up with the Joneses" became popular as consumers tried to outdo one another through home improvements, automobiles, appliances, and fashion. To capture this new consumer dollar, what becomes essential for retailers, manufacturers, and designers is the inclusion of *meanings* and *lifestyles* in advertising related to consumers' dreams and aspirations. This new shift reflected the zeitgeist known as *postmodernism*.

Postmodernism, Philosophy, and Theory

During this time, new ads began to appear, showing clothing that reflected contemporary fashion. With each advertisement trying to vie for the almighty dollar, inspiring branding became key to success. The French philosopher Roland Barthes (Figure 2.7) suggested that advertising was creating a new level of existence for fashion. Barthes, an avid fan of popular culture watching the performances in professional wrestling matches and inspiring fashion shows, developed a theory that has since been called "The Fashion System," which states that a garment is present at three distinct levels: the *real garment* or actual thing; the *terminological garment*, which signifies the primary term, without adjectives, used to describe the object (*T-shirt, jeans, blouse, backpack*); and the *rhetorical written garment*, which includes how the clothing is portrayed and marketed through words, fashion shows, and photographed images (*Abercrombie & Fitch* T-shirt, *Diesel* jeans, *Armani* blouse, *Chanel* suit). Barthes believed that the consumer desires the real garment; however, as his studies helped scholars understand, it was the

Figure 2.7 The author of *The Fashion System* and teacher Roland Barthes, 1915–80. (Photo by James Andanson/Sygma via Getty Images)

rhetorical garment's presentation in photographs (in which the garment is presented to the public either as accurate, as in a fashion show, or manipulated to create a fantasy garment) that is more important for stimulating consumption.[4]

The Jamaican-born British cultural critical theorist Stuart Hall (Figure 2.8) builds upon the work of Roland Barthes with his ideas of what he called "encoding (sender) and decoding (receiver)" of meanings. Hall's multicultural and semiotic approaches to understanding meaning complement Barthes, but with a twist and the incorporation of a multicultural view. For Hall, the *encoding* is the making of a message using a system of coded meanings. For example, how a particular fashion brand creates a visual advertisement with words, images, backdrop, and models. The *decoding* of that message is how a consumer interprets the message or that fashion ad. In other words, how a merchandiser or fashion company creates its product, and depending on our personal worldview, how we will understand it. Think of a time you really connected to a particular product while watching television or a TikTok video. The story of that item is how it was encoded, your relationship to it is how you decoded the message and enjoyed it. How we view and relate to a fashion brand depends on how the brand's story is told to us and on the decoding process. We as individual consumers decode the meaning.[5]

Hall was a multiculturalist and his new theory of communication moving beyond one type of individual to a diverse array of individuals was new at this time. Hall argues that a product's meaning is simply not fixed or determined by the sender (in his case, television media ads). The brand could have multiple meanings because people all think differently. We are multicultural beings and apply our worldview and understanding of a product's use for our own lives. For example, how each of us stylizes a particular garment makes it unique and our own. Again, think how Instagram and TikTok allow influencers to create their

Figure 2.8 Multiculturalist and media theorist Professor Stuart Hall (1932–2014), who gave impetus to the Black arts movement. (Photo by Eamonn McCabe/Popperfoto via Getty Images)

own styles generating multiple outfit variations. This is all encoding and is being decoded by us as we watch and see all the unique looks. And while this is a simplified version of Hall's work, it moves us toward a better understanding of multicultural viewpoints enabling equity among consumer values, not placing one culture above another. Hall believed that there is no ultimate truth or meaning, and that we are at the beginning of a new revolution of consumerism.[6]

Another influential theorist, Jean Baudrillard (Figure 2.9), defines *postmodernism* as a time of simulation. Boundaries between what is real and what is perceived as real have been conflated. This conflation blurs the lines between what an individual knows as reality and what *is* reality, thus causing confusion.[7] The confusion between what is real and attainable versus fantasy is what Baudrillard calls *hyperreality*. Those having *social standing* (Baudrillard's words for people who create fashion brands) at the macro levels of consumer culture create the distortions between reality and hyperreality.[8] Baudrillard contended that the sign (the actual object or image) becomes distorted as it moves through the following stages:

1 It is a reflection of basic reality.
2 It masks and perverts a basic reality.
3 It masks the absence of a basic reality.
4 It bears no relation to any reality whatsoever. It is its own pure simulacrum (simulation).[9]

In the first stage, the object is shown in what Baudrillard calls the natural state; for example, an item is displayed alone without context (verbal or visual presentation). In stage two, the item is aesthetically presented in a context with specific verbal and visual cues that have been created by those of social standing to distort the object and give it

Figure 2.9 Postmodern and hyperreality theorist Professor Jean Baudrillard 1929–2007. (Photo by Ulf Anderson/Getty Images)

new meaning. Stage three represents the absence of all of the object's previous reality; the origins, use, histories, functions, and ideologies of a garment are erased by those of social standing, and it is placed in a fantasy context. In stage four, the object is part of a whole new reality and has almost no relation to its original existence. It is *hyperreal*.

Baudrillard believed that hyperreality is presented to consumers through media. Television, print advertising, computers, hand-held devices, and other forms of communication create hyperreal life situations but introduce them to consumers as if they are real. Airbrushed fashion models in magazines; Instagram pages where individuals conflate their lives to appear better than they are; television shows that display characters never wearing the same clothes twice; distorted lenses on cameras that allow individuals to photograph themselves as either skinnier or more muscular than they are in real life—all of these presentations are appearing to viewers as if they are natural states of being when they are not. For Baudrillard, the methods used by advertisers or individuals to sell products or themselves are examples of hyperreality, and branding reflects these ideas.

Don't believe you ever fell for hyperreality? Have you ever bought the latest iPhone or computer or paid retail for a fashion item? Do you use credit cards to pay for things you cannot afford? Do you drive an expensive car that you really cannot afford? Do you spend lots of money on expensive dinners? Then, yes, you have fallen victim to hyperreality.

Putting It All Together: Rhetorical Fashion, Encoding/Decoding, and Hyperreality

Now that we have examined three major cultural theorists of the twentieth century who reflect postmodern ideology, let us look at how advertising reflects their ideas using a significant advertising campaign. The Maidenform's iconic "I Dreamed" ad campaign launched in 1949 and ran for twenty years. Created by Kitty D'Alessio, each "dream ad" showed a bra-clad female enjoying fantasy activities. Television ads also formed part of this campaign, which was perceived to be cutting edge and risqué for its time. The Maidenform "I Dreamed" campaign is a beautiful example of the shift from the early-twentieth-century advertising ideologies of function to the postmodern era of hyperreality.

The "I Dreamed" campaign also reveals how important branding became to leading US producers for essential items such as underwear until production shifted overseas. The "I Dreamed" campaign reflected the zeitgeist or spirit of the times. It demonstrated how, like Stuart Hall's ideas, a company could create both social and political statements for women by suggesting that their roles in the social order are changing or, in his writings, starting a revolution. Maidenform's ad campaign recognized women's aspirations for everything from working in fashion to stealing the show while wearing their Maidenform bras (see the chapter's opening image). The most ingenious part of the Maidenform "I Dreamed" campaign is that it targeted the segment of the population who were doing most of the shopping during this time: women.

While I encourage you to go out and search for these historical Maidenform ads and discuss them with your friends and colleagues, it is crucial to think about how to *read* these ads. *Reading* is a means of analyzing and critiquing for interpretation. Have you ever heard the phrase "I am going to *read* you?"—meaning that someone is going to critique how you act, look, and dress? In the drag queen culture, *reading* closely evaluates one another's clothes, hair, and makeup to determine who is *real* (looks like a true woman) or who is flawless according to drag standards. But for our purposes, we are examining advertisements for hidden meanings and perhaps messages that are either purposely or subconsciously being portrayed to the viewer. And this aspirational type of play for the consumer is what Roland Barthes believed created consumer desire for the product.

Figure 2.0, a 1960s ad for Maidenform bras, is an excellent example of postmodern advertising, meaning, and rhetorical fashion. This ad illustrates the sheer brand/story about the product.

The viewer is drawn not only to the bra in the center of the photo but also to the woman's glamorous outfit, the trophies, the dog, and various other elements. This photo illustrates a context for selling Maidenform bras. After consumers see the bra, their eyes begin to wander and look at other features. As Stuart Hall would say, you start to analyze or decode what Maidenform has encoded into the ad. Why is she holding that trophy? Why is she (semi)dressed for a cocktail party? Why is there a dog in the photo? What is the ribbon under the dog for? Perhaps she just entered her dog in a show and won first prize? Or maybe she won the talent competition in a beauty pageant by demonstrating dog tricks? Perhaps the dog represents a man since men are sometimes referred to as "dogs," and this ad would then mean a woman is triumphing over men by stealing the show from her "dog." Whatever the case, only after we read the text, "I Dreamed I stole the show in my Maidenform bra," do we realize that the entire event is a dream and not actually happening. It is total fantasy and conflation of reality, or as Baudrillard would tell us, pure hyperreality.

Postmodern Branding Semantics

Jean Baudrillard believed that brands are the principal concept of the new era's culture and constitute a discourse in consumption. He states that "those of social standing have repackaged consumer products in hyperreal scenarios to generate continuous consumption."[10] In turn, those of social standing who use media to create advertising and marketing to sell products are influenced by postmodern popular culture and consumer lifestyles. In the contextual development of postmodern brand cultures, ideas continue to surface; postmodern concepts such as *fragmentation*, *de-differentiation*, *chronology*, and *pastiche* apply to current advertising campaigns. Postmodern theory and branding discourse are part of a contemporary vocabulary and are usually considered standard business semantics. Similarly, as Asa Berger states in *The Portable Postmodernist*, "retailers, marketers, and branding executives incorporate postmodern concepts to create their definitions and meanings of these terms."[11]

Fragmentation describes the separation of similar mass-oriented groupings into smaller, specialized consumer groups and product ranges.[12] In marketing and retailing, such terms as *target market* and *market niche* describe the result of fragmentation. These are the same ideals of Stuart Hall and multiculturalism. These notions of fragmentation reflect a diverse marketplace in which each consumer's taste is unique and individualized.

De-differentiation suggests the blurring of high and low cultures. High culture refers to traditional art practices and what has previously been defined as art, such as couture fashion, sculptures, and paintings. Low culture includes media and items such as comic books, fashion photography, and mass-produced clothes because they serve the masses. These notions of high and low art and culture have been altered in the minds of consumers. New formats, such as graphic design and digital media, are now considered art as well.[13] Concerning fashion, the fuzzy line between fashion-as-art and art-as-fashion is a perfect example of de-differentiation.

For example, retailers such as Ralph Lauren, Gap, Abercrombie & Fitch, and Calvin Klein have commissioned renowned photographic artists Bruce Weber, Herb Ritts, and Albert Watson to shoot their mass-produced clothing such as T-shirts and denim to give them an inventive and creative appearance. Advertising has not historically been viewed as high art, but some critics may have needed to expand their understandings of art after seeing these high-quality images.

Figure 2.10 features the entrance to the Abercrombie & Fitch store. Using Bruce Weber photography, Abercrombie & Fitch's flagship store has created a spectacle that reflects a mix between retail space, nightclub,

Figure 2.10 The Abercrombie & Fitch Fifth Avenue store entrance. Note the two greeters on each side of the door as well as the sizeable photographic poster that suggests an artwork in a museum. (Photo by Mario Tama/Getty Images)

and art gallery. The entryway features two young male greeters on each side of the entrance, suggesting museum guards. The A&F sales associates are stylized to look almost like twins to portray the brand. But what is most interesting is the large-framed image of a male chest in the back center that appears to mimic a work of art in a museum. The spotlighting and the fact that this photo (by Bruce Weber) is prominently displayed in the entryway gives the image an air of being high art and not just a piece of advertising, reflecting de-differentiation notions. The male model in front of the image also helps to draw attention to the poster and at the same time gives the entrance sexual energy.

The term *chronology*, as used by Baudrillard, refers to consumer preoccupation with nostalgia and the past. A consumer may become enchanted with finding what appears to be an *original* item[14] or what appears to be and could be better quality or design. Retailers appeal to these consumers using terms such as *real*, *authentic*, and sometimes even *vintage* to describe products that are knock-offs, new, or of lesser quality. One example would be a Vera Wang wedding dress that Vera Wang made ($125,000) versus a White by Vera Wang ($1,000) for a David's Bridal wedding dress. In this case, the consumer who purchases the latter may be getting a dress that is not designed by Vera Wang at all but is a knock-off of an original; Vera Wang may not even know her name is on the dress! This is all possible because of a licensing agreement that gives David's Bridal the right to manufacture dresses inspired by her work.

Another example is the recent return to heritage clothing by brands such as Levi's® or Shinola, producing "Made in the USA" or "Assembled in the USA" items. Men have an obsession with purchasing garments and accessories that reflect Americana and a time when things were made better because they were made in the United States. Many of these products are sold distressed and washed out to give them the look of heritage clothing. This type of *retro manufacturing* is quite expensive, with Levi's Vintage Made in the USA running at about $300 for a pair of jeans and a Shinola watch at about $675. However, the customers who purchase these items may feel they are buying authentic products because of the price and quality. In both cases, the consumer's purchases are not the *original* unless it is a vintage version or is designed by the designer.

Pastiche, as employed in Baudrillard's thesis, can be defined as collage. In a postmodern consumer culture, pastiche relates to mixing traditional and nontraditional items to create a new context. A great example of pastiche is Instagram accounts, TikTok, and blogs that display individuals wearing clothing in various styles that they have put together. In all these accounts, the owner chooses those individuals' looks and styles they want to show. The mixing and matching of these styles create new individual looks, allowing us to see how various consumers interpret fashion, personally giving each garment a new context. It is the mixing and matching of pieces that create a pastiche.

Hypermodernism and Fashion Forms

Marcia Morgado, a superior fashion scholar, suggests moving away from the postmodern era and into a new era. In her article, "Fashion Phenomena and the Post-Postmodern Condition: Enquiry and Speculation," she identifies major theorists who are calling our new twenty-first-century era by many names, including but not limited to altermodernism, performatism, digimodernism, automodernism, and hypermodernism.[15] In her own words:

> My motivation to write the "Enquiry & Speculation" paper was generated by a textiles and apparel scholar who, on reading my earlier "Coming to Terms with 'Postmodern'" work, wrote to ask: How does fashion reflect post-postmodernism? I was unable to answer this question, and took the query as a challenge to learn. I began by asking what was essentially the same question my colleague had asked of me: How are characteristics

attributed to post-postmodern culture reflected in post-postmodern fashion? I now think I began the 'Inquiry & Speculation' work with the wrong question. A better question would have been: What do apparel scholars and fashion students need to know about post-postmodern culture?[16]

Morgado goes on to state that currently, there is no "best theory" for explaining our current state and era of fashion and consumption. But she feels Lipovetsky's ideas of hypermodernism are a key to understanding our current state of fashion and the connections to consumerism.

In his works, Lipovetsky argues that fashion is a vehicle for the growth and support of cultural values, meaning, and social structures. Clothing has gained meanings that move beyond it just being worn for functional purposes. Fashion now has characteristics and implications such as seduction, irrationality, superficiality, luxury, etc. Lipovetsky uses fashion as a metaphor and the fashion process as a model to describe how commercial practices, products, and services, media techniques and contents, and consumer interests, concerns, behaviors, and identities generate a post-postmodernism mania for overconsumption. He names this emerging cultural change and shift in the era as hypermodernism.

Lipovetsky states that *hyperconsumption*, *hypermodernity*, and *hypernarcissism* characterize the age of hyper. Hyperconsumption is taking hold as we buy more than ever. Causes for hyperconsumption include advertising, branding, consumption websites, digitalization of products, credit systems, and individual ownership. With the use of technology and galloping commercialization, and the growth of excessiveness of everything, we are moving into an era of the shortened product life cycle for consumer goods and a consumer obsession for the new.[17] And consumers partake in the process by purchasing and displaying themselves in the best light to family and friends through access points such as Instagram, Facebook, TikTok, and many other hypernarcissism social networking sites. *How many social media channels do you have?*

In this context, Jean Baudrillard's hyperreality ideologies (remember him a few pages back?) appear as consumers try to live impossibly through aspirations given to them through media and fashion companies. Fashion becomes just one consumer good that is overly purchased and displayed to our friends, families, and those we work with daily, whether face to face or on such virtual platforms as Zoom. Style has become an individualized process as we move into the forthcoming future of how apparel is displayed.

Meaning and Individual Style

Future fashions will create an individualistic perception of each company and its branding techniques for every single consumer. The success of fashion branding will depend on the industry's ability to reflect individuals' styles, making them feel unique. The article "Fashioning Future Fashions," by scholar Gwendolyn O'Neal, notes that fashions (including all body modifications and extensions, such as tattoos and piercings) are restricted and prechosen for individuals by cultural gatekeepers (i.e., retail buyers). However, the individual decides how to blend available elements to craft a pastiche or style, which creates fashion.

O'Neal states, "Fashion does not require the creative genius of an individual which then must be endorsed by cultural gatekeepers, but rather is a process by which individuals continually form and present themselves."[18] She further explains, "Although the body techniques and codes of conduct are imposed by external forces over which individuals have little control, the codes of conduct are acquired abilities of collective and individual practical reason." This does not remove the restrictions of the cultural context but attaches individuals to fashion in order to generate a technique of acculturation.[19]

In O'Neal's view, the acculturation process is not localized but is cross-cultural and transglobal. Media outlets such as television, mobile devices, the internet, and other consumer electronics give consumers immediate access to world events. Fashion trends and styles also unfold almost immediately across the globe through social media such as Facebook, Instagram, TikTok, and Twitter, when previously it may have taken years for fashion to migrate from one nation to another.

O'Neal argues that our world is commercialized and emotional, and she borrows from the futurist philosopher Rolf Jensen when she states, "It will no longer be enough to produce a useful product. A story or legend must be built into it, a story that embodies values beyond utility."[20] O'Neal believes that future fashions will not be limited to objects conceived through the manipulation of creative genius to create a look or mode that is palatable to the masses. Instead, fashion will be constructed in a personal milieu in which the individual manipulates a dress-body complex to create a personal mini-narrative, story, or personal brand of his or her identity. These narratives continue to change and evolve in accordance with specific populations and cultures.

Branding and Consumer Theories

Fashion branding's primary function is to provide a structure that uses images and language to impart meaning to retail products. Whereas an advertiser's primary goal is to sell products, good advertising requires marketers to consider the inherent qualities of products and generate meaning for the consumer. The purpose of advertising is to sell more than just the consumer goods we see in the ads. It connects the consumer and product by providing a *structure*, *method*, and *function* for using the product.[21] These connections generate associations of identity and status in consumer culture. Let's look at how these connections are made by discussing some critical scholars who have researched fashion and consumer behavior.

Context, Consumers, and Meaning

Jean Hamilton, in her article "The Macro-Micro Interface in the Construction of Individual Fashion Forms and Meaning," addresses the transfer of individual fashion forms and their significant meaning from the *macro* (global) interface to the *micro* (individual) level (Figure 2.11). Her study delves into how culture and fashion arbiters globally influence consumers' interpretations of fashion goods and branding ideas. Hamilton touches on how and why merchandise is made and distributed. Her innovative argument focuses on the use of storytelling to create a brand concept and continual consumption.[22] Hamilton's theory suggests that, through storytelling, a context is designed to entice consumers to repurchase mass-produced items.

Hamilton's primary goal is to develop a model based on the notion that macro arbiters influence the micro-level meanings that consumers associate with their personal products. Her theoretical framework illustrates the movement from negotiations with the self (MICRO) to negotiations with others to fashion system arbiters to cultural system arbiters (MACRO).

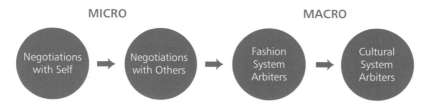

MICRO   MACRO

Negotiations with Self → Negotiations with Others → Fashion System Arbiters → Cultural System Arbiters

Figure 2.11 A rendering of Jean Hamilton's Macro-Micro Interface Model, 1997.

The following list includes the cultural and fashion system arbiters (macro) who underlie this process:

- Designers, product developers, and state planners in controlled economies
- Fashion forms and ideas created by designers and product developers
- The serendipitous (nonconspiratorial) interaction of the components of the delivery (nonconsuming) side of the fashion system; for example, designers, media, producers (including manufacturers), distributors (including retailers)
- The conspiratorial interaction of components in the fashion system: major events and phenomena in the cultural system that influence fashion system participants and institutions as well as individual consumers, such as war, national elections, political revolutions, economic recessions, and depressions
- Trends in the cultural (or subcultural) systems that may influence all or some participants in the fashion system or some individual fashion consumers: for example, Eastern religions, avant-garde music, art, films, literature
- Any or all of the above in combination with one another[23]

Hamilton recognizes the ambivalence of fashion in the postmodern consumerist society, but her article emphasizes the importance of decisions made by the cultural and fashion system arbiters. These decisions serve as persuasive devices for consumers. Because fashion garments carry no meanings and are signifiers only of themselves, it is the arbiters who give them meaning through context and/or display. Moreover, the arbiters must always be aware of what will appeal to a particular consumer or market niche; failure to do so could result in loss of sales.

As Hamilton notes, the QVC (Quality, Value, Convenience) television network connects meaning to consumer goods by displaying them and creating "selling stories" about the products' function and aesthetics. The consumer listens to the story and begins to relate to the item. The item begins to have a meaning associated with it. The consumer feels the need to add it to their collection; this collection of goods serves to establish an individual's identity.[24]

An example of how fashion system arbiters create contextual meaning for products is found in Gwen Stefani's Harajuku Lovers "Pop Electric," which debuted on HSN (Home Shopping Network) on October 16, 2014 (Figure 2.12). HSN and QVC have databases of information about previous customers who have purchased similar lines. They also know

Figure 2.12 Multi-platinum singer, songwriter, and fashion entrepreneur Gwen Stefani shares a moment with HSN host Amy Morrison (L) during the worldwide launch of Gwen's new Harajuku Lovers Pop Electric collection of fragrances at HSN studios on October 16, 2014 in St. Petersburg, Florida. A reinvention of her wildly popular Harajuku Lovers line, the Pop Electric collection is available exclusively via HSN TV, hsn.com, and HSN Mobile. (Photo by Tim Boyles/Getty Images for HSN)

what previous scripted segments for these types of product lines sell the most products. Therefore, when Gwen Stefani discussed her fragrance line and referred to topics that were familiar to her fans, she enticed them to buy. While she was on the air, she listened and talked to callers (customers) who had previously purchased her other products. The callers told Stefani and others who watched the show how they wore or used Stefani's other fragrances and items. Anyone watching this might have related to the conversation and wanted to purchase the products because they were hearing and watching it. In this example, "Pop Electric" becomes the signified product through the selling context of HSN that gives it meaning and creates a story for its uses and promotion. Without the context, the product might not sell or be enticing to consumers.

In his article "Texture and Taboo: The Tyranny of Texture and Ease in the J.Crew Catalog," Matthew Debord discusses the relevance of J.Crew's reinvention of mail-order catalog sales in the postmodern era. By creating retail catalogs that depict hyperreal lifestyles, J.Crew entices consumers to purchase basic products that they probably already own. According to Debord, the catalog has become a work of art that creates an aura of exclusiveness and allows consumers to shop from the privacy of their own homes (both using the catalog and online). The catalog has created lifestyles that are fantasized and almost surreal.[25] Since Debord's study, the J.Crew catalog has continued to present models in fantasy settings, creating a visually perceived relaxed attitude. Debord's contextual analysis is significant because he can recognize a retailer's talent to create meanings and fantasy associated with mass apparel for selling to consumers.

Debord takes an art critic's view when discussing J.Crew's contextual marketing techniques. He makes no qualms about his frustration with J.Crew's manipulation of what he believes are disappointing and insignificant fashions.[26] He does not admire the company's ability to generate revenue by creating an entire fantasy lifestyle advertising campaign. But while Debord takes a negative view of J.Crew's tactics, they do have redeeming qualities. The clothing marketed in J.Crew's catalog reflects mass fashion at its most practical. Reasonable prices and the garments' classic styling and versatility mean that they can virtually be worn until they wear out. The advertising strategy and lifestyle stories within J.Crew's catalog reflects postmodern culture. Using a cultural context, the company attaches meaning to its products through the technique of brand/story.

A Short Brand/Story

Future Consumption of Brands: Interview with Lorynn Divita

Dr. Lorynn Divita is an Associate Professor of Apparel Merchandising at Baylor University in Waco, Texas. She is the author of the textbooks *Fashion Forecasting* (Bloomsbury) and the upcoming revised edition of *The Why of the Buy* (Bloomsbury). Dr. Divita has been interviewed about fashion trends for various national media outlets, presented her research at academic conferences, and consulted on fashion forecasting topics for industry clients.

Where do you see the future of consumer behavior and fashion brands?

With so many retailers and brands declaring bankruptcy recently, it's evident that the old apparel industry mindset of "pile it high and watch it fly" is no longer feasible. It's no longer just about the clothes because a lot of clothing out there is indistinguishable. Customers are pressed for time and faced with an overwhelming number of options, so if they know they consistently connect with a few key brands, that edits their choices down to a manageable number. Brands that don't lose sight of what it is about them that resonates explicitly with their target market will be able to weather the storm.

You are a noted author concerning the future of fashion trends and forecasting. How do you see branding impacting these areas?

Branding can help consumers bridge the gap between their actual selves and their ideal selves. As fashion industry professionals, sometimes it is easy to lose sight that most consumers are only vaguely aware of macro-level changes in styles and instead rely on favorite brands to help keep them looking current. If a consumer likes a brand, and that brand introduces a new trend, the consumer is more likely to think, "Okay, this must be a thing," overseeing the same trend from a brand they don't know or care about purchasing.

In your opinion, what do the best brands do to beat out their competitors? Is being on social media important?

Consumers now have para-social relationships with brands or the feeling that brands are friends; how many times have we heard someone say, "Oh, I just love Gucci SO much!" as if the brand were a person? Brands cultivate this perceived relationship and make their customers feel "seen" through their social media presence, maintaining constant communication with their customers and deliberately choosing images, messaging, and endorsers that they know will appeal to them.

What should consumers be aware of when lured in by a good brand/story? And what advice would you give consumers when they shop for brands?

Thanks to technology, we are in the era of transparency. Consumers have heard about brands that boast of empowering their workers who might have toxic workplace environments or brands that promote their sustainable practices later exposed as greenwashing. And brands that say they stand for ethical manufacturing that ultimately are found to have unsafe working conditions. Any brand that promotes its values as a critical part of its identity had better have the receipts.

My advice to any consumer would be to figure out what is important to you and then shop accordingly. If you decide that social responsibility is essential to you, it is easier than ever to learn about a company's values. If a brand says they stand for something and later revealed they don't walk the walk, there are plenty of other options out there that will align with your values without sacrificing style.

Cultural Branding Theories

Douglas B. Holt of the University of Oxford developed the concept of *cultural branding*. Cultural branding addresses the individuality of the consumer. According to Holt, cultural branding is the future of all businesses that sell products and services to consumers. His concept of cultural branding is branding "derived from brands that have spun such compelling myths that they have become cultural icons."

> Cultural branding applies particularly to categories in which people tend to value products as a means of self-expression ... Marketers usually refer to these categories as lifestyle, image, badge, or ego-expressive products ... managers can apply these lessons of cultural branding to any market offering that people regularly use, or else idealize as a means to improve their lives.[27]

According to Holt, cultural activists study popular culture and then develop successful brands. These brand leaders assemble cultural knowledge rather than worrying about traditional consumer research. Instead of analyzing numbers and looking at spreadsheets, these experts come to understand those individuals who live in the cultural context.[28] This cultural knowledge is developed in the following ways:

- Examining the role of major social categories of class, sex, gender, and ethnicity in identity construction rather than obscuring these categories by sorting people into "psychographic" groups

- Viewing the brand as a historical actor in society
- Viewing people holistically, seeking to understand what gives their lives meaning, rather than treating mass culture simply as trends and entertainment.[29]

To succeed, cultural brands must reflect an appropriate market and develop a product's identity. They must also be consistently reinvented when the marketplace changes as a reflection of popular culture. The marketplace determines the eventual success or failure of any brand.

Holt suggests looking at consumers as individuals instead of target markets. Smaller companies who depend on individual clients to maintain their business usually take this approach and examine each person's characteristics. Those involved in the individuality of clients must evolve their companies along with changes in the marketplace. Successful fashion brands become attachments to the customer's lifestyle and create the perception that they are personalized to each individual. As a result, the consumer does not feel like a member of a mass population but rather as unique and special.

Think Gucci (Figure 2.13), where consumers are treated exceptionally well as this brand sells products above the average price point. Even those who cannot afford Gucci are attracted to the brand's ideology, being an established Italian company known for high-quality products. Purchasing

Figure 2.13 Gucci Store located in London's Heathrow Airport. (Photo by author)

a Gucci belt, loafers, and even one of their signature handbags gives an individual a feeling of owning part of an elitist heritage entrenched in perceived quality fashion. After all, when someone spots the Gucci "G" they know the consumer has spent a lot on the product, even if they had to charge it on a credit card.

The same can be true of mass retail companies that understand the historical equity of their products—basics such as polo shirts, khakis, jeans, and dress shirts—well enough to appreciate the most advantageous product positioning. For example, Ralph Lauren's various divisions (Polo at Macy's, Purple Label at Saks, and Chap's at Kohl's) reach different cultural markets while reflecting a consistent Ralph Lauren brand message. Vera Wang has used the cultural institution of marriage to turn her company into a conglomerate that demonstrates an understanding of her target market and the needs of individuals.

These brands have become what Holt calls *iconic fashion brands*, which develop culturally contextual stories that consumers can understand and embrace. This is what makes them successful. Holt believes these brands accrue two complementary assets: cultural authority and political authority:

> When a brand tells stories that people find valuable, it earns the authority to tell similar kinds of myths (cultural authority) to address the identity of a smaller constituency (political authority) in the future. Specifying brand's cultural and political authority provides managers directions to develop myths for the brand and allows them to rule out myths that are a poor fit.[30]

In the following few chapters, *Fashion Brand Stories* will show you how each brand in this book has become accepted in the cultural context and marketplace. For example, Ralph Lauren and Vera Wang have established brands in our culture, but are they the best for their particular product categories? The stories that have been created about these brands emphasize who they are; however, some consumers may feel that these companies make inferior products. Nevertheless, the brand myths and product reputations of Ralph Lauren and Vera Wang allow them to maintain a competitive edge in the marketplace. These two brands are powerhouses supported by millions of dollars.

Storytelling and Success Brands

Author and branding expert Laurence Vincent supports Douglas Holt's notions of using brand myths and narratives (stories) to create positive brand culture. Vincent defines a brand myth as a traditional story of ostensibly historical events that unfold part of people's worldview or explain a practice, belief, or phenomenon. The occidental mythology of ancient civilizations helped explain the mysterious workings of the natural world through stories about God and heroes' struggles and conquests. Today, brand mythology serves a similar purpose. Scientific discovery answered many of the mysteries of the natural world. Still, it has not satisfactorily resolved the complex questions we have about social existence, sense of self, and our relationship with the world. Brand mythology has curiously interceded. Like ancient mythology, it works through narrative devices.[31]

In his book *Legendary Brands: Unleashing the Power of Storytelling to Create a Winning Market Strategy*, Vincent highlights the success of Levi's and Starbucks (Figure 2.14). He reveals how each company established a brand culture through stories, creating the perception that the brands are superior. Also, each fashion brand situates itself within popular culture in the hope of becoming part of the social order and cultural context—in other words, a permanent fixture in the big scheme of the world. Can you picture a world without Levi's or Starbucks?[32] Levi's and Starbucks culturally integrate themselves within each environment, wherever they have stores, by becoming part of the city and its culture. For example, Starbucks in Heathrow Airport is probably quite different from the local one closest to you.

Figure 2.14 Starbucks Coffee, located in the center of London's Heathrow Airport terminal, serves unique products not available at all locations. (Photo courtesy of author)

According to Vincent, there are four parts of a brand narrative: plot, character, theme, and aesthetics.[33] Aesthetics includes any part of the brand that stimulates one of the five senses. Spectacle (what you see), song (what you hear musically), and diction (how words are constructed to convey meaning) are essential elements for visual and performing arts. Brands, however, can also stimulate taste, smell, and touch, and these can be powerful devices.[34] For example, entering a store of a retailer like Starbucks, you hear music, smell coffee, touch products, and see all kinds of people in addition to brand baristas that serve you. Making a connection to the consumer through this sort of brand narrative is key to success. The description must relate to the consumer both culturally and personally, and the consumer must develop an attachment to the brand based on the narrative. (Otherwise, the consumer may leave without purchasing anything.)

Vincent further states that through brand narratives, a symbiotic relationship between the consumer and the brand must occur for the consumer to identify with the brand. Whether experienced in a store or through an advertising campaign, the brand narrative must get attention so that audience members can follow the characters used in the brand advertising and marketing campaign.[35] For example, the use of Audrey Hepburn in Gap's September 2006 advertising campaign for slim pants created a narrative that most consumers could relate to in their own lives. The consumer may have associated with Gap, Audrey Hepburn, her movies, or just "her total beatnik look" from the images used in the windows and the television commercial. Consumers unfamiliar with Audrey Hepburn might have been interested in the song "Back in Black" sung by AC/DC or might have investigated further to understand the ad's cultural significance and meaning. Whatever the case, this connection to Hepburn built brand recognition and created a narrative for Gap to perhaps build consumer loyalty (you can see it on YouTube).

Sometimes words and actions are not needed; as the old saying goes, "a picture is worth a thousand words" or, for fashion branding, thousands of dollars. One brand that has been known for using a combination of few words and great photography is Calvin Klein. Since the early 1980s, Calvin Klein ads have communicated narratives to consumers that keep them returning for more of the company's products (Figure 2.15). Placing terrifically sculpted models in contemporary and surreal settings, Calvin Klein delivers a consistent image that has made him a fashion brand icon—sex! A 2009 Calvin Klein billboard stirred up so much controversy that even New York City officials questioned if it should come down. Like other Klein billboards, this one stopped traffic as it suggested a

Figure 2.15 Pedestrians on a sidewalk near a Calvin Klein billboard on the side of a building June 17, 2009 in the SoHo neighborhood of New York City. The provocative ad featuring a topless model and three young men provoked controversy in the city. (Photo by Chris Hondros/Getty Images)

sexual fantasy between three men and one woman. But the advertising remained (after all, it is New York City), allowing Klein sales success among his already dedicated followers.

Lifestyle Merchandising and Emotional Meanings

The former *Wall Street Journal* reporter Teri Agins (Figure 2.16) reveals in her book *The End of Fashion* that the survival of designers and retailers is dependent on their proficiency in branding their consumables. Fashion, according to Agins, is not about products but rather about how they are marketed and sold as a "brand image," or what she calls *lifestyle merchandising*. Whereas garments such as T-shirts, khaki pants, and jeans are staples found in many of our closets, what makes them unique or special is their meaning through branding campaigns. This phenomenon suggests that although clothing is an essential component of popular culture, the actual garment itself has become secondary to the branding techniques used to sell it. Her work is a landmark for its time, although Agins is neglected as a critical scholar of fashion. She traces and tells the stories of Emanuel Ungaro's likes, his major makeover, Giorgio Armani's impact on Hollywood, and how even designers like Zoran remained

Figure 2.16 Wall Street Journal columnist Teri Agins at the David Rubenstein Atrium at Lincoln Center on February 8, 2011 in New York City. (Photo by Andrew H. Walker/Getty Images)

true to himself. Agins describes Isaac Mizrahi's descent, refusing to do mass fashion until he went bankrupt but then saved by Target through a significant licensing deal. This book allows us to see how and why so many high-end couture designers had to go into mainstream fashion.

Agins reveals the success of designers such as Ralph Lauren, Tommy Hilfiger, Donna Karan, and Calvin Klein in lifestyle merchandising. While Lauren was repackaging the polo shirt, Hilfiger was reinventing the Oxford shirt, and Karan was creating new women's apparel; but it was Calvin Klein who rebranded denim jeans. He may well be the man you can blame for paying high prices today for jeans such as True Religion, Seven for Mankind, and Diesel. Klein's 1980 advertising campaign featuring a fifteen-year-old Brooke Shields stole the show. Shields became embroiled in the central controversy of Klein's jean ads. More importantly, consumers responded to this ad campaign by scavenging department stores searching for Calvin Klein jeans. The designer jeans craze was launched, and Calvin Klein had branded himself and his name as the king of denim jeans. He had created mass hysteria over denim and generated an emotional response from consumers across the nation.[36]

In *Emotional Branding*, the late Marc Gobé points out that successful fashion brands can capture their customers' emotions and personal convictions. Gobé states, "Corporations need to fine-tune their focus on the consumer psyche and understand the importance of the constantly evolving trends in their consumers' lifestyles."[37] He believes that it will be the norm for retailers to brand according to their specific target markets; companies that make emotional ties to consumers will rise to the top, whereas those who do not will fall.

Another researcher who has continually focused on a meaning related to fashion branding is Grant McCracken. His research emphasizes that studying clothing is essential to understanding the cultural evolution of society. According to McCracken, meaning moves continually from the "culturally constituted world" to the gatekeepers of consumer goods to individual consumers; all three add meaning to a brand as it passes through their domains. McCracken's theory suggests that through social interactions, individuals (and eventually society) assign status to fashion-branded garments and types of consumer goods.[38]

McCracken's research connects meaning to brand management. He emphasizes the need for brands to be studied using a meaning-based method instead of traditional information and statistical analysis. For the development of the consumer market, meaning will become more effective in determining consumer consumption patterns. According to McCracken, fashion marketing is one key to the creation and generation of future consumer consumption.[39]

McCracken identifies nine different types of meaning targeted by companies: gender; lifestyle; decade; age; class and status; occupation; time and place; value; and fad, fashion, and trend.[40] These meanings are determined by the company, its competitors and collaborators, customers, marketing segmentation, product and service, positioning, market mix, and the price of each consumer item.[41] He suggests that fashion branding students should study the various types of meaning used to create context around consumer goods. By examining all aspects of a company, individual consumers can see how the fashion branding story reflects products and services.

A Short Brand/Story	Scouting Future Fashion and Patterns: Interview with Krista Lowther

Krista Lowther served as the Director of Strategic Patterning Services and Innovation for L Brands. She graduated from Ohio University with a BS in Merchandising and from The Ohio State University with an MS in Textiles & Clothing, focusing on women, sports, and fitness. Her career spans over twenty-eight years working for L Brands, parent company to Victoria's Secret, VSX, PINK, Henri Bendel, Bath and Body Works and Express. In her tenure at Express, Lowther was also an Associate in Planning and Allocations, Merchandise Testing, and as an Assistant Buyer.

Tell a little bit about yourself

My whole career I have worked in the retail and fashion industry, I have a BS from Ohio University and my MS from the Ohio State University. My first job out of college was as an assistant buyer, then briefly in positions in planning and allocation at Express. After five years with Express, I decided to get my MS. After I completed my postgraduate degree I worked freelance for several years with a fashion website for a large corporation. Eventually, I was hired onto the Strategic Patterning team in charge of process and planning.

What is an average day for you?

Retail doesn't usually have an average day. Especially when one of the keys to success is moving quickly, you never have the same day twice. Every day is something new, you can have a priority when you arrive at the office, and by 10 a.m. that is no longer of any importance to the company or brand and they are totally interested in researching a completely new fashion concept or product. And no matter how high you are on the career ladder, there is always the administrative piece to the job, phone calls, emails, meetings, etc. But the focus of the day you won't know till it is all over.

Do you think the fashion market is becoming more competitive?

Yes, definitely, in a lot of ways. Now it isn't only about getting new merchandise and fashions into stores and the customer's hands quickly. There is a digital avenue and the competition with start-up companies, small business, and worldwide accessibility for anything the customer might want. Sustainability awareness is making vintage and second-hand outlets more popular. Gone are the days of taking clothing to a resale shop. Now you can just send a bag to Thread Up, then they post and sell them on the internet for you. It is a much wider audience.

What is scouting?

Scouting is about being curious, inquisitive, and looking for innovation and outside-the-box ideas that can drive the bottom line of the business, creating new products, categories, or outlets.

What are the components of scouting?

You have to be curious about the where, why, how, etc. You have to want to do the research and think outside the box. For fashion you need to shop the furniture show to know what direction the colors are trending. Go to CES (a technical trade show) and see what is happening there. Then you need to be able to share that new concept or idea, then present the details in a well thought-out way with the others in your business, so they can see the potential as well. Then as a team agree on an implementation strategy that helps make the idea a success.

Why is it important?

Scouting is important to be able to do "next" better and faster than anyone else in the fashion market. You can get practically anything from anywhere if you are looking for it. For the average consumer, they wait till it comes to them, so you need to deliver a product that is timely and affordable, that is brand right with everything else in your store. It should supply something your customer wants, but did not even know she needed till she saw it.

How do you decide if a trend is important to follow or not?

I think it is more about knowing your customer and if she/he is interested. There are so many trends happening in the world and there is a place for many of them. But you need to know your customers, likes, dislikes, price point, etc. Customers want newness and freshness in your assortment but they still need to know they are in the same store. Too much of a pendulum swing and you might lose them. Patterning is about identifying trends and innovation, the design and merchant teams are important in editing to make sure it is brand right.

What is patterning?

Patterning is searching the world, both real and online, to find a consistent repeating idea i.e., pattern or direction. Consumers in other markets can be early adapters but making sure it translates well in your market is of equal importance. COVID 19 has created a huge upswing in active, lounge, and casual to a level we have never seen before. Patterning is also great for new concepts of retailing, for example Amazon's Go and with walk-out shopping. This sort of technology could translate to just about any business model.

What are the elements of patterning?

Patterning is very detail oriented and analytical. You will follow and report on every aspect of a store or category of merchandise in the exact same way for a period of time to see the trend. Kind of like the stock market, if you follow it long enough you begin to see the highs and lows.

How crucial is it to understand your competition's patterns of behavior in planning future business?

You can learn a lot from someone else's mistakes, as well as their successes. You must keep an eye on what is happening around you and how that might influence your business or your customers' choices.

Where do you think the future of scouting and patterning for hot brands is going?

The world is faster, people are smarter and focus on what they want, what they believe in and stand for. As retailers being ever curious about the market as well as the world about you is key. You must remain fast and ahead of the competition and that gap is closing for a lot of specialty retailers with mass market stores like Target collaborating with designers worldwide. Having the network of people on the ground in key cities who understand your business and focus is more important than ever. Again, with COVID-19 and travel restrictions, how do you know what is happening in Paris, London, or Tokyo without a set of eyes there to keep you informed and up to speed?

Shifting Views and Consumers Speaking Out

When asked about the future of theories related to fashion branding, one can cite Ecclesiastes 1:9 and 1:10 and the words of King Solomon: "What has been will be again, what has been done will be done again; there is nothing new under the sun," and "Is there anything of which one can say, 'Look! This is something new?' It was here already, long ago; it was here before our time." And while not being religious, I feel there are no more valid words. After all, why say what has already been said before?

Fashion is cyclical, and theoretical understandings are no exception to the rule. While we have rising social media such as Instagram and TikTok, print magazines are still here (the media of early and mid-twentieth-century theorists). More interesting, television shopping (QVC and HSN) was thought only to be an innovation of the late 1980s and early 1990s that would die out in the age of the computer. However, it has remained strong even with the rise of other forms of virtual shopping. No longer do consumers watch just on television, they now watch QVC and HSN on their devices, with both channels doing phenomenal business. We can say the internet is no longer innovative, with consumers relying on it as a norm. And the COVID-19 pandemic saw almost 55 percent of consumers going online to purchase goods and services they would have traditionally purchased in brick-and-mortar outlets.[42]

And we are starting to see that while Chinese and Japanese consumers like shopping via access points (APS) on their smartphones, consumers in the United States still prefer to shop brick-and-mortar and online. We see brands such as Amazon that start online building stores, indicating that brick-and-mortar stores are still important. The future will not be a single channel of retail, and those who are putting all the initiatives into just digital retailing will need to ensure their success through multiple means of shopping. The future for brands is to be everything to everyone through the store, television, e-commerce, kiosk, social media sites, fulfillment anywhere, returns anywhere, and the same price across all channels.

But *Fashion Brand Stories* is about individuals and their relationships to brands. This book is intended to challenge your mind *and not in the numerical sense*. In a world of retail analytics and data points of consumerism, this book is to get you thinking about storytelling through all types of retailing strategies and enables you as the reader to see how relationships are being conceptualized and theorized to various brands. But, practically, is the future of branding how well brands relate to individuals?

The world is changing, and consumers are no longer the same as those who purchased goods thirty, twenty, even ten years ago. Let us take a look at the largest consumer market in the world, the United States. According to the US Census Bureau:

> Between 2014 and 2060, the U.S. population is projected to increase from 319 million to 417 million, reaching 400 million in 2051. The U.S. population is projected to grow more slowly in future decades than in the recent past, as these projections assume that fertility rates will continue to decline and that there will be a modest decline in the overall rate of net international migration. By 2030, one in five Americans is projected to be 65 and over; by 2044, more than half of all Americans are projected to belong to a minority group (any group other than non-Hispanic White alone); and by 2060, nearly one in five of the nation's total population is projected to be foreign-born.[43]

And while everyone reading this book may not be a US citizen, it is crucial to understand that these findings represent a significant population shift in the one country that consumes the most and represents a diverse consumer market.

The Census Bureau indicates that consumers are becoming more ethnically diverse. This is happening right now. In contemporary popular culture, ethnic minorities and those of mixed backgrounds are leading changes, assuming positions for the first time. For example, the Vice President of the United States, for the first time, is a multi-racial woman, Kamala Harris, born to an Indian mother, Shyamala Gopalan, and British Jamaican Black father, Donald Harris, and was raised in Oakland, California. Her husband, Douglas Emhoff, is our first Second Husband (usually Second Lady) of the United States. This couple represents our country's future with a contemporary attitude toward mixed-race marriages (Figure 2.17).

We also see shifts in attitudes about culture and celebrate the world's holidays. The Chinese New Year is now more visible than ever before, with retailers across the United States doing visual displays to celebrate (Figure 2.18). During the 2018 Year of the Dog, Macy's in Herald Square erected a tree in honor of the celebration in the middle of the cosmetics department, one of the store's most visible sections. Retailers such as Macy's, Coach, and others now offer product lines in homage to the holiday to attract Chinese consumers. Even more, the celebration of this holiday has now built awareness among other shoppers who may not even have been aware of it and when it occurred each year. *Do you know your Chinese zodiac sign?*

Figure 2.17 Democratic Vice President Kamala Harris and her husband Douglas Emhoff appear on stage after Harris delivered her acceptance speech on the third night of the Democratic National Convention at the Chase Center in Wilmington, Delaware on August 19, 2020. Harris is the first African American, first Asian American, to win the vice presidential office on a major party ticket. (Photo by Win McNamee/Getty Images)

Figure 2.18 A tree in Macy's Herald Square store in New York City celebrates the 2018 Chinese New Year. (Photo courtesy of author)

Figure 2.19 The Empire State Building in New York City hosts the cast of *RuPaul's Drag Race All Stars* on December 4, 2018. (Photo by John Lamparski/Getty Images)

Another shift in culture is illustrated by the growing acceptance of same-sex marriage. This has changed the economic and social climate, as more and more gays and lesbians are coming out. Our attitudes concerning those individuals have changed thanks to the pioneering efforts of television shows like *RuPaul's Drag Race* (Figure 2.19), which, at the time of writing, has thirteen seasons. While some critical cultural theorists might scrutinize the performance and commercialization, it has normalized issues surrounding being gay, crossdressing, race, and gender. The show has gotten global exposure, with those in Middle Eastern Countries now calling for gay, lesbian, and transgender rights.

Issues of gender continue to change as top personalities tell the world that there are not just males and females but also people with fluid gender. *Gender fluid* consumers mix what has been called traditional masculine and feminine characteristics and may switch back and forth between these appearances depending on the weekday. For example, the rise of young men using cosmetics has allowed them to accentuate what might be viewed as a traditionally feminine look because we are not used to seeing men in makeup. But this behavior is becoming somewhat normative among younger generations of men who do not see anything wrong with wearing cosmetics and who use them daily.

Being gender fluid has nothing to do with what set of genitalia one has or what one's sexual orientation is. It is all about appearance, not who one dates. This appearance and the ability to relate to a new

Figure 2.20 Laverne Cox and Geena Rocero attend the 29th Annual GLAAD Media Awards at The Hilton Midtown in New York City on May 5, 2018. (Photo by Jason Merritt/Getty Images for GLAAD)

demographic of consumers who refuse to honor traditional gender boundaries indicate that the older era has been shaped to a new type of gender fluidity, allowing individuals to appear however they want. And *transgender* is no longer a shocking word, thanks to the pioneering efforts of such fabulous celebrities as Laverne Cox and Geena Rocero (Figure 2.20).

Laverne Cox made her first national appearance on the television series *Orange Is the New Black*, in which she portrayed the transgender character Sophia Burset in prison. Cox is the first transgender person to appear on the cover of *Time* magazine, has gained the respect of gay, lesbian, bisexual, and transgender communities, and has received accolades from peers in the television and motion picture industries. And Manila-born Filipino supermodel Geena Rocero has appeared on the cover of *Harper's Bazaar* and speaks avidly in her TED talks about transgender rights. Rocero was the first transgender Playboy Playmate of the Month for 2019.

But we are still a world obsessed with being thin and being perfect. Women's body sizes are still the subject of bullying and will continue to be a significant issue for the future of fashion and branding. Some companies still refuse to cater for plus sizes or what is now standard

Figure 2.21 Ashley Graham and husband Justin Ervin in Avignon, France, June 28, 2019. (Photo by Arnold Jerocki/G.C. Image)

sizing (XS–2XL) for women. But big-box retailers, like Target and Macy's, serve this customer in style. And while both men and women in this target market have to pay more for their clothes, women such as the famous fashion model Ashley Graham (Figure 2.21) continue to battle for women of all sizes, declaring that all women have the right to fashion. Graham discusses body image issues and how girls should be encouraged to accept their body types and not be forced to feel ashamed. After all, we all come in different shapes and sizes. Fashion needs to get over it because most consumers have—let us hope fashion starts listening.

Another market fashion brands will see becoming more visible in the future is people with disabilities. The most recent eye-opening and pop-cultural experience portrayed to the public is the remarkable feats of Columbian designer Guio Di Colombia who, during Medellin Fashion Week in Columbia, featured models from all walks of life, including two landmine victims (Figure 2.22). From survivors of war to wheelchair users, Di Colombia's show celebrated those that fashion often forgets. But this was not just a one-time gesture as this designer continues to use models with disabilities in all his shows, gaining him the respect of this community as an advocate for them.

Figure 2.22 Landmine victim models walk behind Colombian designer Guio Di Colombia (R) at Colombiamoda during Medellin Fashion Week in Medellin, Colombia, on July 24, 2019. (Photo by JOAQUIN SARMIENTO/AFP via Getty Images)

But what does all this have to do with fashion branding? A lot. Because it will be the duty of retailers, the merchandisers referred to as those "editors of fashion" that theorists Gwendolyn O'Neal talked about, to ensure that these communities' choices are there for them to construct their personal milieu and buy those fashions that relate to them as consumers. More importantly, it will be fashion brands' responsibility to create memorable brand/stories that include these individuals in their ads.

The more we are becoming inclusive, the further we seem to become segregated through the likes of digital media that do not force us to *expand our knowledge* and see the world as it is by going outside. Instead, we watch it virtually and experience one another through access points like Instagram, TikTok, Twitter, and Facebook. I believe that consumers need to get out more and experience all the brand/stories they can for themselves, and not just read about them or experience them virtually or on television. It is our duty as individuals to see what we can see and experience things firsthand. In the words of the famous film character Mame Dennis-Burnside, "Life is a banquet, and most poor suckers are starving to death, live … live … live!"[44]

ed in this chapter? Back up your research with
re a report for your colleagues.

olving to suit the new attitudes and lifestyles
e. Trace the history of a brand using a multi-
has this brand evolved its stores, website, printed
cial media, and ads? How is it portrayed across
unication? Is this brand telling an unforgettable
hy not? What are some suggestions you have for
aper, including images, and share your ideas with

ration

Fashion Films on Vimeo (2011), https://vimeo.com/
films

d of Fashion (New York: William Morrow, 1999).
he Language of Fashion (London: Bloomsbury, 2004).
esentations: Cultural Representations and Signifying Practices
e Publications,1997).
., Jean Baudrillard: Selected Writings (Stanford, CA: Stanford
ress, 1988).

m

5. Na
   and
   Who
   might

6. Find a Tv
   dedicated
   colleagues.
   web page.

of our
channel appro
marketing in stores,
all channels of comm
brand/story? Why or
this brand? Write a
your colleagues.

Further Explo

Watch:
Álvaro de la Herrán
channels/fashio

Read:
Teri Agins, The Er
Roland Barthes,
Stuart Hall, Repr
(London: Sac
Mark Poster, e
University P

Chapter 3
Democratization of Merchandising: Ralph Lauren

Chapter Objectives

> Explain the importance of lifestyle merchandising as a branding strategy
> Review the significance of a concept designer
> Emphasize the importance of a clothing selling context when branding fashion apparel
> Examine the growth of Ralph Lauren as a global lifestyle brand

Figure 3.0 Ralph Lauren, Oprah Winfrey and Ricky Lauren. (Photo by Dimitrios Kambouris/ Wirelmage)

When considering *lifestyle merchandising*,[1] the name Ralph Lauren stands out. He has borrowed functional military garments, such as cargo pants and duffle coats, and traditional work clothes from Americana such as canvas barn jackets and blue jeans and transformed them into luxury garments that sell for thousands of dollars. Lauren's method is known as lifestyle merchandising, which builds associations and gives historically practical garments an elevation to the luxury market. By placing mass fashion garments in luxury settings, Lauren redefines them and gives them a new identity. This image leads consumers to associate Ralph Lauren products with high-end status. From a single concept for selling ties to the 2011 launch of Denim & Supply, Ralph Lauren has displayed a brand image that is aspirational and classically iconic with an attitude uniquely its own for baby boomers and X, Y, and now the millennial generations (Figure 3.1).

Ralph Lauren has dedicated over forty years to the creation of his brand image. His lines are featured on fashion runways and in every department store across the nation. But contrary to popular belief, Ralph Lauren is not a traditional designer; he is a merchandiser—a concept designer. Lauren is the *conceptual design* genius behind his brand, not the person who drafts patterns, sews strips of fabric, or sits behind the computer-aided design software program. Instead, he goes out and finds vintage garments, antiques, and other historically relevant items and steers his team into recreating that particular item in the manner

Figure 3.1 An interior view of the new Ralph Lauren store at Via Montenapoleone in Milan, Italy. (Photo by Giuseppe Cacace/Getty Images)

that should be Ralph Lauren. As the king of merchandising, he has total creative license to dream up ideas that influence his brand. *For example, how do you sell a pair of ripped-up and paint-splattered painter's pants for $400?* His biography is a component of his brand; without Lauren, the man, the garments are worthless. Lauren has maintained control over every aspect of his business so that it perfectly reflects his vision.

There have been many articles and books written about Ralph Lauren. Recently, he published an autobiography about his ascent to the top of his field.[2] *Ralph Lauren* presents a glamorous life and highlights all of Lauren's wonderful accomplishments. Some biographies, such as *Genuine Authentic* by Michael Gross, are not always so complementary,[3] whereas others, such as *Ralph Lauren: The Man, the Vision, the Style*,[4] make him out to be a hero, a man among men. It is important to consider both sides when reading this chapter, as the main purpose is not to critique Ralph Lauren from a personal perspective but to highlight his growth as a lifestyle merchandising and branding powerhouse.

History of a Merchandiser

Ralph Lauren was born on October 14, 1939, the son of Russian Jewish immigrants. His real name was Ralph Lifshitz, but in his late teens, he and his brothers had their names changed to Lauren. He had a normal childhood, with a modest upbringing. He grew up in the Bronx and lived with his parents in a two-bedroom apartment. He shared a room with his brothers throughout his childhood and often wore their hand-me-down clothes. He became accustomed to the worn look of the garments and eventually enjoyed the style of the apparel. The casual look of the Ralph Lauren line would later reflect nostalgia for his childhood.

Young Lauren purchased clothes from the Army/Navy surplus store, Alexander's discount store, and Discount of the Day. He enjoyed these clothes because he knew no one else would own them.[5] According to most biographers, his personal appearance became an obsession. He became infatuated with his body, skin and, most obviously, his clothes.[6]

Although Lauren never finished college, he did attend City College of New York for two years. His first retail position was at Brooks Brothers in men's furnishings in the late 1950s. In the mid-1960s, he took a position with Boston-based tie manufacturer Rivetz. Sources indicate that while he was an average salesman, his appearance management was extraordinary.[7] He believed that by dressing in a particular style, he would be iconic in the manufacturing business. He utilized self-promotion as a way to stand above his peers and get attention from clients. Lauren's unique style allowed him to gain sales and a stylistic reputation. Whereas some thought his appearance was unusual, others viewed him as a genius. He became skilled at networking in the New York garment district. He learned early on that building relationships was essential to creating his own brand.

The Polo Line

After attending a polo match and seeing the opulent lifestyle associated with the sport, Lauren put "the cart in front of the horse" and created the name of his product line—Polo—before any of the actual products. To Lauren, brand image was everything. In 1967, Beau Brummel, the Cincinnati-based tie firm, gave Lauren an opportunity to launch his own line of ties by looking beyond the fashion trends of the time. His concept was to sell wider ties with a larger knot at the top. During a time when ties were only 2 to 3 inches wide, his ties measured 4 inches across (Figure 3.2).

Figure 3.2 Designer Ralph Lauren showing off his tie on January 1, 1970. (Photo by Jack Robinson/Hulton Archive/Getty Images)

Lauren also sold his ties at higher prices than the competition. To him, if the price was higher the client would perceive that the quality was better. During this time, *Playboy* and the menswear periodical *Daily News Record* (*DNR*) featured articles about Lauren's new ties. The title of the article in *DNR* was "The Big Knot."[8] This article attracted interest from buyers for Bloomingdale's and other high-end retailers. After his line of ties was established, from 1968 to 1969 Lauren expanded his Polo menswear line. Conceptualizing the perfect in-store presentation for his product, Lauren opened the first men's shop-within-a-shop for his collection at Bloomingdale's in New York City.[9]

In 1971, Lauren established a line of tailored shirts for women, based on the cut of men's suits. That same year, he debuted the Ralph Lauren women's shop-within-a-shop at Bloomingdale's and introduced the Polo player logo on his product lines.[10] He also opened his first store on Rodeo Drive in Beverly Hills. Jerry Magnin, whose great-grandfather started the luxury department store I. Magnin, financed the store. This was quite an accomplishment for a young merchant who had been in the business for only five years or so. This store was the first freestanding store for an American designer brand. By 1980 there were seven more stores in the Ralph Lauren chain, in Fort Lauderdale, Atlanta, Houston, Detroit, Chicago, Palm Beach, and Dallas.[11] In 1972, the Polo logo shirt was introduced in twenty-four colors. The marketing campaign stated, "Every team has its color—Polo has 24."[12] Ralph Lauren merchandise was now sold in exclusive stores such as Bloomingdale's, Neiman Marcus, and Saks Fifth Avenue.[13]

Lauren hosted his first women's fashion line during this time, and although the clothing line was hailed as extremely stylish, the fit of the garments was horrible. Instead of using standard-size models, Lauren used his wife Ricki Lauren and colleague Buffy Birrittella as size models for the garments. Both were svelte and trim, had very little cleavage and were a size 2. Most customers were unable to even fit their arms into the sleeves of the women's Oxford shirts. These sizing issues were eventually remedied.[14] Lauren continued to create menswear, women's wear, and accessories over the next several years. Then his brand's exposure was increased through the motion picture industry.

Films and Fragrance

In 1974, Ralph Lauren's design style became recognized around the world through the release of *The Great Gatsby*, starring Robert Redford (Figure 3.3) and Mia Farrow. Although most of the garments for the

Figure 3.3 Robert Redford leaning against a luxurious car in a scene from the film *The Great Gatsby*, 1974. (Photo by Paramount/Getty Images)

movie were actually styled and constructed by costume designer Theoni V. Aldredge, Lauren inspired the men's garments. Aldredge won the Oscar for the costumes and was even asked to sell her fashion designs from the movies at the Bloomingdale's store in New York.

In 1976, Lauren received his second Coty award for women's wear and was inducted into the Coty Hall of Fame for menswear.[15] By this time, Ralph Lauren had established himself as a key figure in American design. To expand his business, Lauren launched his Polo line for boys in major department stores. The line reflected his menswear, complete with ties, blazers, khakis, and Oxford shirts bearing the embroidered polo player.

In 1977, with the assistance of costume designer Ruth Morley, Ralph Lauren received honorable mention in another motion picture by providing the clothes for Diane Keaton and Woody Allen in the movie *Annie Hall*. With the launch of this film, a trend for eclectic combinations such as classics with vintage style became popular in men's and women's clothing. For the film, both Woody Allen and Diane Keaton wore Lauren's current fashion line (Figure 3.4).[16]

In 1978, Ralph Lauren launched a line inspired by the American West. Author Colin McDowell states that it "hailed [Lauren] as the man who 'recaptured' America for America and it rebuffs the erroneous impression that Ralph Lauren's fashion is too British."[17] With the launch of the

Figure 3.4 Diane Keaton and Woody Allen in the film *Annie Hall*. (Photo Courtesy of Bettmann)

Western product line, Lauren decided to become part of his brand image by posing in ads. By modeling his own products, he began to create the image that he was authentically Western. Even though he had never been a real cowboy (but has since become one), Lauren began to create the reality that surrounded his childhood fantasies of cowboys living on ranches. In the same year Ralph Lauren also launched his first fragrances, Lauren for women and Polo for men. It was the first time that a brand introduced both a men's and women's fragrance at the same time.[18]

These two fragrances enabled Lauren to enter a new niche market of consumers who perhaps were avid fragrance and grooming purchasers but not necessarily familiar with Lauren's clothing line. The distinct scent of leather, wood, tobacco, basil, and oakmoss makes the Polo brand immediately identifiable. The floral (violet, carnation, rose) and wood spice of Lauren for women is also quite distinct. These two fragrances are still popular. The company even created an 8-ounce spray bottle (which is very uncommon) of Polo for those who are obsessed with the fragrance.

Redefining the Lifestyle and Going Global

In 1979, Lauren refreshed his image with a unique twenty-page marketing campaign using photographs by fashion photographer Bruce Weber in national magazines. As described by author Colin McDowell,

"The ads featured little or no text, frequently using non-models, in which the clothes are seen as part of an overall lifestyle. The results, almost cinematic in breadth, captured the public imagination and have been frequently copied."[19]

The ads firmly established Lauren as a lifestyle brand. The popularity of the Weber photographs helped Ralph Lauren become an international fashion mogul. With captions such as "Rough wear—it was made to be worn," the ad campaign was the model for today's lifestyle brand advertising. These ads inspired companies such as Abercrombie & Fitch, which also used Weber photographs to create its lifestyle advertising campaigns.

In 1981 Lauren debuted his Santa Fe collection, which influenced his designs throughout that decade and continue to be seen in his collection. The collection was recognized by the international community as a substantial contribution to the world of fashion because it was the first to introduce the theme of the American West to high-end fashion. Ralph Lauren became known as the company that created the authentic spirit of America by using fashions inspired by the Western frontier. The fashion line continues to be significant in the United States and Europe. The Santa Fe collection generated an upscale image of Ralph Lauren

Figure 3.5 Ralph Lauren shop in Old Bond Street London, August 14, 2005. (Photo by Jamie Tregidgo/WireImage)

as a lifestyle brand that presented a particular image of Americans to international markets. It romanticized the American West, establishing an image of American fashion with cowboy boots and hats, Western shirts, denim jeans, big buckle belts, rawhide fringe jackets, prairie shirts, flannel shirts, and thermal Henleys. The Westernwear frenzy crossed the ocean in 1981 with the opening of the Ralph Lauren store on Bond Street in London. The store was an instant success. Ralph Lauren was now the first American design company to have its own European boutique (Figure 3.5).

A Short Brand/Story   ## Luxury Branding: Interview with David Loranger

David Loranger, PhD, spent seventeen years in New York City working in the design and luxury retailing industries. Loranger worked for Bergdorf Goodman, Barneys, Loro Piana, and Saks Fifth Avenue. He is currently teaching Fashion Merchandising in Welch College of Business and Technology at Sacred Heart University in Fairfield, Connecticut. Dr. Loranger teaches courses in buying and merchandising, luxury retailing, and design thinking. David holds a doctorate from Iowa State University in Apparel, Merchandising, and Design in addition to a Master's from the Fashion Institute of Technology in Global Fashion Management. His research foci are on cultural apparel products and generational marketing and consumption.

What is happening with luxury brands? Are they still luxury?

Bernard Arnault is really the one who changed luxury forever. His focus on operations and production management shifted the whole focus of the luxury industry from high-quality products that are made in limited quantities to mass production. Luxury companies cannot realize double-digit growth every year without extending their brand and the consumer base. It's by compromising both quality and exclusivity that they appeal to a broader range of consumers who would not normally be luxury consumers. They convince these "masstige" consumers that they're luxury consumers by letting them buy into accessible parts of the brand. This is why these days a customer will pay $90,000 for a Mercedes or BMW made in Alabama. The "masstige" consumer who buys luxury brands now doesn't even have the awareness to know that the luxury product that they're buying is actually made in the United States. Louis Vuitton makes in Encino California. This is a roundabout way of saying most luxury brands in the world are not true luxury anymore. They will try to convince you that they have "redefined what luxury is" to be more accessible and democratic to everyone—but how is something exclusive and luxurious when everyone has it? Luxury is luxury by sheer virtual fact of scarcity, quality, exclusivity, and the fact that only a certain few are informed enough to appreciate a true luxury item.

Where do you see the future of luxury branding?

Whether or not luxury brands return to the old way of exclusivity and scarcity, the future will definitely include sustainability and technology. I think that's the really huge focus of luxury brands going into the future. Whether it's infusion of technology into product, social media, or in-store technology, this will be the way that luxury brands will connect with their consumers and develop a relationship. This is especially important considering that brands are eager to connect with younger Millennials and Gen Z consumers … and soon they will also want to connect with Alpha consumers. In terms of our more contemporary understanding of sustainability being defined as saving people and planet for future generations, it's currently being realized by Kering. The number of brands that Kering has that focus on sustainability in terms of those Triple Bottom Line issues is quite impressive and they are indeed a leader in the luxury industry. I think sustainability will combine with technology to expand our definition of triple bottom line in terms of 3-D printing, bio textiles, and reuse and upcycling. I think a real opportunity for fashion brands in the future will revolve around vintage repurposing, such as the The Real Real and Depop. I think that luxury brands are really missing out on an opportunity by not creating their own platforms to verify product authenticity and to resell it to consumers. The ultimate expression of the future will be that the luxury brand will turn into a co-customization interface

(Continued)

and the consumer will assume the manufacturing [of] the product. What I mean by that is that you will go on to, let's say, Louis Vuitton's or Gucci's website, you will co-design a product there, and then you will be able to 3-D print it right in your home!

Why are luxury brands so important to our consumer climate?

I don't immediately recall who said it in the movie, but in *Scatter My Ashes at Bergdorf* (2013, Fortissimo Films), one of the commenters says that luxury brands are important because people need to have some type of point of reference to know when they have actually attained success. They also need a set of products to consume to represent that success and also to enjoy that success. In a way luxury brands are important because they serve as a North Star of what it means to achieve success. On the other hand, luxury brands are important in a real economic and material culture sense. Companies like Hermès have bought smaller companies that would have failed long ago merely because they uphold a specific and precious material culture tradition in terms of making. It's only through the beneficence of companies like Hermès that the smaller companies that produce silver, Limoges china, furniture, essences, and other inputs to the luxury industry have existed and continue to exist. Puiforcot, John Lobb, and Saint Louis are examples of this. Handicraft and makers, and luxury as an industry all go hand in hand. It's really important that we maintain these material culture traditions, because once they are gone they are gone forever.

Out of all the luxury brands, for you, which one tells the best brand/story?

I think everybody pretty much knows what I'm about to say. For me Hermès is the one and only true luxury brand left in the world. Hermès is living proof that you don't have to compromise on quality or exclusivity or preciousness or the mystery of the brand in order to grow and be successful. Hermès has had a consistent brand story throughout [its] history and has evolved, changing with the times to be able to be relevant for consumers at every stage of the company's lifetime. The thing that really stands out about Hermès is the creativity and the endless pursuit of maintaining and improving their craft, innovating in terms of design inspiration and materials, tirelessly maintaining and refining their experience in an omni-channel sense. This is what sets the brand apart from the rest of the luxury brands of the world. Most luxury brands around today try to maintain a patina of what Hermès does in reality every day, but they fail miserably because the focus is merely on profit instead of making the consumer happy with extraordinary products and services. The consumer and the product are at the center of everything that Hermès does and that's what makes them exceed expectations every time. Luxury brands should take a cue from Hermès and realize that it's more sustainable and meaningful to do a specific thing exceedingly well, than to try to do a number of things with mediocrity.

The Empire Grows

Lauren's company continued to flourish, launching new product lines, expanding into the international market, creating award-winning fragrances, and sharing the wealth through philanthropic efforts. Its success is a result of networking, creative thinking, a focus on increasing public awareness, strategy, and most importantly, a clear vision for the brand—a consistent lifestyle image and story.

Ralph Lauren Home, *Out of Africa*, and the New York Flagship Store

To expand his merchandising empire, Lauren next turned his attention to products for the home.[20] The venture would extend the Lauren lifestyle into the consumer's home environment. The ads for the three home design lines—Log Cabin, Thoroughbred, and New England—displayed images of traditional home furnishings with a rugged twist and simply stated "How Tradition Begins." Each line had its own branded message. Log Cabin reflected a luxury cowboy suite, and Thoroughbred was reflective of an English country house.[21]

In 1984 Ralph Lauren's design concepts appear to have been influenced by the movie *Out of Africa*, which starred Meryl Streep and Robert Redford. Lauren had remained friends with Redford since *The Great Gatsby*. *Out of Africa* was in preproduction when Lauren released his line of traditional safari styles with the rugged and worn style that is now synonymous with Ralph Lauren. Many of Lauren's ads during this time looked as if they were mimicking stills from the movie.

In 1986, Ralph Lauren opened his flagship store in New York City in a building that was previously a mansion belonging to the Rhinelander family (who never lived in it). The building, located on Madison Avenue at 72nd Street, was completely renovated. The store was to become a Ralph Lauren masterpiece, reflecting everything the Ralph Lauren brand stood for in the mind of the consumer (Figure 3.6). The first Ralph Lauren boutique in Paris also opened that year.

Figure 3.6 The Rhinelander Mansion in New York. (Photo courtesy of author, all rights reserved)

From Exotic Fragrances to the Rugby Store

In 1990, the Lauren image of high quality and luxury extended to yet another award-winning set of fragrances with the launch of Safari for both men and women. It was the first lifestyle fragrance that was merchandised with a range of accessories and home furnishings to complement it. The Safari fragrance won the coveted Fragrance Foundation's FiFi award for Fragrances Star of the Year in 1990 and again in 1991. The Romance fragrance for women was launched in 1998 and received the FiFi Fragrance Star of the Year award and the Best National Advertising Campaign award. Romance for men soon followed and received both awards in 1999.

In the early 1990s, RL Jeans Company and the Polo Sport Line were launched with a store opening in 1993 at 888 Madison Avenue, across the street from the Rhinelander store (which has since become a women's mansion store). RL Jeans Company and the Polo Sport brand marked a change in the advertising style of Ralph Lauren, as well as a shift in the target market for the company. It was during this campaign that Jamaican model Tyson Beckford (Figure 3.7) became the leading male model for Ralph Lauren. Prior to the launch of Polo Sport, Lauren had used primarily Caucasian models in his ad campaigns. Beckford's face would be the new look of Ralph Lauren over the next few years, appearing in ads for the fragrance Polo Sport, for underwear, and eventually for the Purple Label division.

By using Beckford in his ads, Lauren made a strong statement concerning diversity and the concept of lifestyle merchandising to the global market. At this time, rappers, hip-hop artists, and other black celebrities were wearing baggy clothes. MTV and VH-1 played videos of these stars wearing baggy Ralph Lauren stylized clothing with their underwear waistbands exposed. The looks started influencing street fashions. Lauren knew this market had significant spending power and would purchase his clothes. Beckford's face and the ads for Polo Ralph Lauren underwear and Polo Sport would connect the brand with relatable markets. With both these less expensive lines, new consumers would emerge: Polo Sport was cut, designed, and fitted in a baggy silhouette reflective of the streetwear of the time, and Polo Ralph Lauren underwear had a lower pricepoint, allowing those who normally could not afford Ralph Lauren to own a part of the brand.

In 1993, Lauren introduced the Double RL line, named after his Colorado ranch (Figure 3.8). Double RL, sometimes referred to as RRL, reflected a romanticized heritage lifestyle of military men, men's tailoring,

Figure 3.7 Supermodels Bridget Hall and Tyson Beckford launch Polo Jeans Company's new creation called "easy rides" at Macy's, August 22, 1996 in New York City. Beckford represents the Polo Sports line exclusively and Hall has a Ralph Lauren and Maybelline contract. (Photo by Evan Agostini/Liaison)

and the cowboy. Flannel shirts, denim jeans, cargo pants, military shirts, and traditional-cut suiting reflected the styles worn on TV shows such as *Bonanza*, *Hogan's Heroes*, and *Downton Abbey*. The line carried a hefty price point, with most garments appearing as if they had been worn for years (think very high-end grunge with cowboy hats, leather bags, and silver accessories). This look was one of Lauren's favorites, with form-fitting cuts that reflected his personal style (see Figure 1.1 in Chapter 1)

Ralph Lauren Purple Label debuted in 1994 with its line of men's tailored and custom clothing. This advertising campaign also featured Ralph Lauren as the model. The clothing was made from finer fabrics with a tailored silhouette, and the line was introduced when casual Fridays became all the rage in the business sector. This line was designed to bring custom-made garments to the retail sector.[22]

Lauren added paints to his home goods line in 1995, continuing the lifestyle branding messages his company had built over the years. The colors ranged from Gray Flannel, Suede, and River Rock to Duchesse Stain.[23] The paints added a finishing touch to the look of his home furnishings brands.

Figure 3.8 Ralph Lauren Double RL Company Store in New York's Nolita Area. (Courtesy of the author)

In 1996, Polo Sport Women was introduced and won the FiFi award for Best National Advertising Campaign. This moderately priced women's collection was reminiscent of the traditionally tailored Polo-style line that Lauren had created in the early 1970s. This division of the Polo brand became Lauren's better women's sportswear line in all major department stores.[24]

In 1997, Polo Sport launched the RLX line of authentic high-tech sports clothing. And Ralph Lauren opened his first restaurant adjacent to the Chicago flagship in 1999. That same year, Polo Ralph Lauren acquired Canadian specialty retailer Club Monaco.[25] Known for its sleek and narrow fashion assortment in basic colors, Club Monaco continues to operate in locations in the United States and Canada.

RalphLauren.com was launched in 2000, allowing consumers to buy merchandise on the web. Eventually the "Create Your Own" feature was added to the website, as well as an online magazine called *RL Magazine*. During the 2002/3 fashion season, Lauren creations were shown on the runways in Milan; the Purple Label line for men was shown in the spring along with the women's Blue Label line; and the company's first children's-only store opened on Madison Avenue. It was the first freestanding children's wear store, featuring the same quality and style of the Polo brand line.

Ralph Lauren's Rugby division, dedicated to Generation Y, was launched in 2004. The Rugby line represented a nostalgic look at the Ivy League experience and the ideals of a collegiate setting. Shoppers understood the preppy look with a twist; unlike his competitors, who identified this look with icons such as whales, alligators, and ducks, Lauren used the skull-and-crossbones for the Rugby product line. Rugby associates wore dreadlocks, colored hair, tattoos, and even body piercings, unlike the crisp, clean look of those found at Polo Ralph Lauren or competitors such as Abercrombie & Fitch or American Eagle, who were targeting the same market.

Some critics have stated that Rugby was Ralph Lauren's response to the popularity of Abercrombie & Fitch. However, this author disagrees. The product assortment in the Rugby line was more European than that found at Abercrombie & Fitch, and the stores' ambiance was completely different. But in 2011, Rugby was closed and replaced with Ralph Lauren's new line for young hipsters called Denim & Supply. Denim & Supply, found exclusively at Denim & Supply stores and Macy's, shifted from an Ivy League look to an inner-city hipster look with a mix of grunge, artistic style, and historicism. Like its predecessors Polo Sport and Rugby, it was a hit with the young college and high-school crowd at a price point they could afford. The division closed after a successful run.

Innovation and Scrutiny

Ralph Lauren continued his brand's global awareness by opening flagship stores in Moscow (2007) and Hong Kong (2014). While opening the Hong Kong location Lauren globally launched his Polo Red cologne signifying good luck and happiness in Chinese culture. An extremely noteworthy achievement has included his use of *4D technology* to cast fashion shows on his flagship store in New York to celebrate a decade of technology and innovation (Figure 3.9). The show stopped pedestrians and onlookers in their tracks, demonstrating that, while this was an established brand, it was still reflective of the presence of new technologies for presenting fashion.

Lauren repeated this strategy when he launched the new Polo Ralph Lauren line for women in 2014 to salute the new store on Fifth Avenue. He has become the man associated with sponsoring US Olympic athletes and outfitting them in the finest apparel, and he sponsored the television show *Downton Abbey* in 2013.

Figure 3.9 External view of the RalphLauren.com 10 Years of Innovation with 4D Light Show at the Ralph Lauren Madison Avenue Store on November 10, 2010 in New York. (Photo by Henry S. Dziekan III/Getty Images for Ralph Lauren)

But the brand as not been all success, as Ralph Lauren's use of Native American (First Nations People of North America) has been scrutinized by those who believe the brand practices cultural appropriation. The term signifies the use of another culture without giving proper context or credit to the people from which it originates. In 2014, Refinery 29 reported the brand had inappropriately imbedded images of the First Nations People of North America in its Ralph Lauren RRL line. Activists across the nation used the #BoycottRalphLauren on Twitter and other social media outlets. The brand quickly apologized for this travesty and has since made amends. But Lauren's brand is not the only one to use such imagery as the lines between what is appropriate and inappropriate start to blur. In 2014, Pharrell appeared on the cover of Elle wearing a First Nations People headdress, for which he too apologized.[26]

Philanthropy and Stardom

The standard of excellence associated with Lauren and his company has been recognized repeatedly. In 1992, Ralph Lauren received the Council of Fashion Designers of America (CFDA) Lifetime Achievement award, one of four top honors he has received from the organization over the years. In 1997 Polo Ralph Lauren became a publicly traded company on the New York Stock Exchange, and in 2000 Ralph Lauren was inducted into the Fashion Walk of Fame in New York.

Lauren's philanthropic endeavors are well known. The man loves people. In 1993 Polo Sport fragrance sponsored the first annual Race to Deliver. This event raised funds for the charitable organization God's Love We Deliver, which provides hot meals for housebound people with HIV/AIDS.[27] Ralph Lauren has also been a huge contributor to the 7th on Sale charity for HIV/AIDS. The brand supported Pride in London by painting a building in Shoreditch in the rainbow flag colors on June 26, 2019. The first Gay Pride Rally was held in London on July 1, 1972 to commemorate the anniversary of the USA Stonewall riots of 1969. Pride London was formed in 2004 and is now known as Pride in London. It celebrates the diversity of the lesbian, gay, bisexual, and trans+ (LGBT+) community with a parade and festival and is widely supported by businesses and organizations across the city (Figure 3.10).

Ralph Lauren's support for breast cancer campaigns was rewarded with the first Humanitarian award from the Nina Hyde Center for Breast Cancer,[28] which was presented to Lauren by Lady Diana, Princess of Wales. In 2000, RalphLauren.com donated $6 million to establish the Ralph Lauren Center for Cancer Care and Prevention at North General Hospital in Harlem, and the Pink Pony campaign donates 10 percent of all proceeds from that line to cancer research and awareness programs.

Figure 3.10 Ralph Lauren supports Pride in London by painting a building in Shoreditch in the rainbow flag colors. (Photo by Quintina Valero/Getty Images)

Lauren's commitment to the arts and education was recognized by Brandeis University with an honorary doctorate of letters. In 1998, a corporate gift of $13 million from Ralph Lauren went to the Save America's Treasures Campaign to help preserve the flag that inspired Francis Scott Key's "The Star-Spangled Banner." In the wake of the World Trade Center attack on September 11, 2001, Lauren established the American Heroes Fund, raising $4 million for the relief effort and scholarship fund for children of victims. He continued his community relations with a $110,000 donation to the Abyssinian Church of Harlem. The church thanked Lauren with an award given by *Vogue* magazine's André Leon Talley, who stated:

> What Michelangelo was to the Sistine Chapel, what Carl Sandberg was to the American iambic pentameter, and what F. Scott Fitzgerald was to the grammar of the American romance story, Ralph Lauren is to American Style. His vision, his commitment to excellence, his incredible style and grace, his elegance, his profound philanthropic spirit speaks volumes for this great leader and man.[29]

Discussion Questions

1. Explain the difference between a traditional designer and a concept designer.
2. Where did Ralph Lauren work prior to working for himself? Why do you think this experience was beneficial to his career?
3. Currently, how many divisions does Ralph Lauren operate under his name? Can you identify the target market of each division? Are they homogeneous or diverse?
4. Why was Ralph Lauren's use of an ethnic model such as Tyson Beckford important for social justice? Does the fashion industry use enough ethnically diverse models? Why or why not? Give examples.
5. How has Ralph Lauren built on his original Polo Ralph Lauren brand to create an empire and an almost unparalleled career in fashion? Can you think of any other merchandisers with similar backgrounds?
6. Why is philanthropy important? How does philanthropy strengthen a brand presence?

Expand Your Knowledge

Most retailers and brands have established an image for themselves by using lifestyle merchandising as a strategy for selling their products. Go out to the shopping district, local mall, or shopping center and identify two stores (maybe your favorite stores) that sell very similar or identical products. How does each of these retailers contextualize the products differently to give them a different lifestyle presence? For example, how does each of these stores sell a similar product like jeans? Do they merchandise them the same way? Outfit them with similar garments? Have the same store fixtures? Use the same type of in-store marketing? Price the garment the same? Do sales associates wear the garment the same way? Does the store play music or have a fragrant smell? Record your results and report what you find.

Further Exploration

Watch:
Bloomberg Quicktake, *Ralph Lauren: How I Built a Fashion Empire* (2015), https://www.youtube.com/watch?v=WTqYMoz_inU (accessed April 25, 2021).
Read:
Alan Flusser, *Ralph Lauren: In His Own Words* (New York: Abrams, 2019).
Ralph Lauren, *Ralph Lauren* (New York: Rizzoli, 2017).

Chapter 4
Rebel Brand Style: Vivienne Westwood

Chapter Objectives

> Discuss the brand/story of Vivienne Westwood
> Examine her crossover between music and fashion
> Define a subcultural leadership model and Westwood's impact
> Describe the ideology and rebel nature of Westwood as a spokesperson on rebellion

Figure 4.0 Designer Vivienne Westwood and her husband Andreas Kronthaler attend the Life Ball 2014 at City Hall in Vienna, Austria on May 31, 2014. (Photo by Gisela Schober/ Getty Images)

If there is anyone who can take subcultural and radical style and turn it into prêt-a-porter fashion, it is Dame Vivienne Westwood. She is the godmother of punk style and has had a career that spans over forty-five years. There are many things you may not know about Westwood; her brand/story is unique. She was a teacher, is a mother and a grandmother, and has created a distinctive fashion empire built on her own morals and principles. She is not afraid to take chances and welcomes challenges.

Westwood is considered an icon and a fashion veteran. She has received the highest accolades throughout her career, including the British Fashion Council's British Designer of the Year, 1990 and 1991; the British Government's Most Excellent Order of the British Empire, 1992; Dame Commander of the Most Excellent Order of the British Empire; and an Outstanding Achievement award at the British Fashion Awards, 2007.[1]

Westwood's style reflects the antiestablishment and the aesthetics of radicalism. With her iconic historical collections such as Pirates (1981), Witches (1983), and even Clint Eastwood (1984), it is clear she does not go with the flow and that her approach is matchless. Her designs reject the traditional standards of dress and have often been inspired by radical street styles with wild swing influences. Using everything from leather and rubber fetishism, punk rock, and sexual bondage to a blatant embrace of homosexuality, she incorporates themes into her designs during eras when others would have found them to be just too risqué. When Westwood did her collection in 1994, she incorporated the return of the bustle by placing fanny pillows under just about everything and announced the butt to be the new erogenous zone.[2]

Like most designers, Westwood has seen weak financial times, but she continues to be brand-strong by continuing to show in Paris, and her style is mimicked by other designers and retailers. She has done many outside jobs; she was a professor of design at the University of Berlin, and in 2011 she was featured on the Canadian television show *Vivienne Westwood's London*. Her works also extend into corporate enterprises: she recently designed the uniforms for Virgin Atlantic.[3]

Westwood has become a spokesperson for sustainability and the fight against global warming. She spreads the word about not buying fast fashion, encouraging consumers to buy clothes that will last longer. She has gone to Nairobi to help launch her collaboration with the Ethical Fashion Initiative. With the help of local villagers in the Nairobi region, she is creating wonderful tote bags from scraps of material found in landfill.[4] Westwood has remained one of the classiest queens of fashion, while remaining humble. She is a true global citizen who is challenging the norms and trying to save our planet one day at a time.

A Marriage of Music and Fashion

Vivienne Isabel Swire was born on April 8, 1941, in Glossop, Derbyshire, to Dora and Gordon Swire. She has a younger sister, Olga Swire, and a younger brother, Gordon Swire. Vivienne learned to sew at a young age and always made her own clothes so that she could save her money to buy expensive and nice shoes. After attending Harrow Art School for one term, she married Derek Westwood at twenty-one and turned her hand to primary teaching. In 1963, Vivienne's first child, Benjamin Arthur Westwood, was born. In 1965, Vivienne's first marriage ended after her brother introduced her to Malcolm Edwards (McLaren), and in 1967 they had a son named Joseph Ferdinand Corré.

In 1971, Vivienne's career in retailing and fashion began when she and Malcolm opened their first shop at 430 King's Road and called it "Let it Rock." In 1972, they changed the name of the shop to "Too Fast to Live, Too Young to Die." In 1973, Vivienne traveled to New York for the first time with Malcolm McLaren,[5] when she became extremely interested in punk fashion. The look included bondage and sadomasochism (BDSM) fashion, safety pins, razor blades, bicycle or lavatory chains on clothing, and spiked dog collars for jewelry. Hair and makeup were done in overexaggerated styles. Punk fashion also included the enculturation of Scottish design with the use of tartan fabric.

Upon her return from New York in 1973, Vivienne Westwood and Malcolm McLaren changed the name of their shop to SEX. Vivienne began to design and make clothes for such celebrities as the rock band New York Dolls.

In the landmark year 1975, McLaren created the historically famous punk band The Sex Pistols, while Westwood was arrested for exhibiting and displaying indecent materials. Their new SEX shop was sprayed with pornographic graffiti, adorned with rubber curtains, and merchandised and inventoried with all-in-one body suits, leather miniskirts, chains, padlocks, fishnets, stilettos, and leather underwear. This underground boutique was the hidden subcultural place to shop.[6]

The SEX shop was a place for outcasts and those who did not fit in with the norms of British fashion and style. It brought with it a new era of antifashion that would soon become iconic and associated with Westwood for the rest of her life: punk fashion.

In 1976, McLaren and Westwood again changed the name of SEX to Seditionaries. During this time Westwood started producing her famous bondage trousers using black sateen or wool. These pants were an instant success, and many found them to be comfortable and emancipating.

Westwood also created straight jacket-inspired shirts out of muslin fabric that were stenciled in red, black, and white with an off-center neck hole. These creations added to the punk aesthetic, reinforcing the identity of what it meant to dress in this style. Seditionaries became not only a retail store but also a space where punks could hang out and socialize. It was immersed in the punk lifestyle.[7] In 1979, Seditionaries changed its name to World's End.

In the early 1980s, while Malcolm McLaren's interest was primarily music and Westwood's fashion, the two collaborated to create styles for retail buyers and sold them in their store. The first collection (Figure 4.1). that was shown was Pirates (1981), featuring swashbuckling clothes of dandies, highwaymen, buccaneers, and pirates (Figure 4.2). Westwood and McLaren spared no expense, using the likes of famous pop star models such as Nick Kamen to display the garments. While Westwood did most of her research by using historical analysis, McLaren was inspired by the streets. Together they created successful contemporary fashion while borrowing from both historicism and street style.

The Pirate collection was sold at the World's End boutique and was promoted through Malcolm McLaren's band Bow Wow Wow in their music video *C30, C60, C90, Go!* Another great celebrity at the time, Adam Ant, wore Vivienne Westwood's collection and "Apache" Native American makeup suggested by Malcolm McLaren in his 1981 music video *Stand and Deliver*. This look became the signature style associated

Figure 4.1 Vivienne Westwood and Malcolm McLaren at her fashion show at Olympia, London, October 22, 1981. (Photo by Brendan Monks/Mirrorpix/Getty Images)

Figure 4.2 Vivienne Westwood World's End Fashion show "Pirates," Autumn/Winter 1981–82, the first catwalk show of Vivienne Westwood and Malcolm McLaren, at Olympia, London, October 22, 1981. Male model Nick Kamen featured in the center. (Photo by David Corio/Redferns)

with Adam and the Ants and even inspires his look today (Figure 4.3). This combined use of runway shows, retail stores, and 1980s music videos might make Westwood and McLaren the first fashion design team to promote garments using a multichannel presence.

At this time, since purchasing the latest MTV video styles was not easy, many young high-school kids and college students had to make clothes to look like the latest music videos. Westwood contributed to music fashion styles and was willing to be known as a designer to musicians of various genres, including punk, new romanticism, and new wave. At a time when many designers would not choose to have their latest creations emulated by subcultural music genres, Westwood was proud to do so.

In 1982 Westwood and McLaren launched the collection Savage, which was inspired by Native American geometric patterns: saddlebags, leather frock coats, foreign legion hats worn back-to-front with eye slits, soft leather bag boots, bowler hats with padded headbands to give them an oversized look, "petti-drawers," and shorts. Fashion models were stylized with body paint and mud plastered into their hair. While Westwood did most of the fashion work, she gave credit to McLaren.[8]

The third collection (1982–3) was called Buffalo, sometimes referred to as "Nostalgia of Mud." For these designs, Westwood was inspired by exotic elements of global dress along with Rastafarian elements (think Bob Marley

Figure 4.3 1981 British pop sensation Adam and the Ants, comprising of, from bottom clockwise, Adam Ant, Merrick, Marco Pirroni, Terry Lee Maill, Gary Tibbs. (Photo by Hulton Archive/Getty Images)

and dreadlocks). The results included items borrowing from large tunic-style African dresses, paired with Dominican hats, Peruvian beads, and tribal-like makeup. The look reflected a postmodern pastiche island mentality that was perceived as quite fashionable for the time,[9] with sheepskin jackets, twisted and asymmetrical cuts using tattered materials, fall-down socks, fabric-covered boots, huge felt "Mountain" hats with dents (which are still sold today) and big swirling layered skirts. The look was very popular with McLaren, who used it to market his music along with the World's Famous Supreme Team, who sang their hit song "Buffalo Gals."[10]

In 1983, the new collection Punkature was launched, to be followed by Witches (1983–4). Vivienne has stated that she went to New York to visit the artist Keith Haring to buy some of his art because of its use of fluorescent fonts with dark backgrounds and hieroglyphics (think the 1980s video game Space Invaders). Vivienne felt that Haring's work was almost magical and a type of esoteric language. The Witches collection was a mix of cream-colored waterproof cotton mackintoshes, knitted jacquard body suits, and tube skirts in washed-out navy blue and fluorescent pink. With the end of Witches in 1984, McLaren and Westwood ended their collaboration.

A Short Brand/Story	Queer and Punk Influence on Brands: Interview with Marvin Taylor

The punk scene is an example of a subcultural style that has become a global fashion movement. The punks of the 1970s are aging and moving on in life. But it is important to discuss what it was really like during this time with people who know. The gay, lesbian, bisexual, and transgender communities played a role in the era of punk. Some identified as queer and still do today. Marvin Taylor, the former director of the Fales Library in New York, is one of them and an expert on the subject.

Taylor holds a BA in Comparative Literature, an MLS from Indiana University, and an MA in English from New York University. He has held positions at the Lilly Library at Indiana University and at Columbia University in the Rare Book and Manuscript Library, as well as their Health Sciences Library. He has been at the Fales Library since 1993. In 2013, Taylor was promoted to full curator, the first librarian to be promoted to this rank in the history of New York University.

Currently, Marvin Taylor is Curator for Food Studies and the Arts.

In 1994 Taylor founded the Downtown Collection, which contains over 12,000 printed books, 18,000 linear feet of manuscripts and archives, and 90,000 media elements. He was editor of *The Downtown Book: The New York Art Scene, 1974–1984* (Princeton University Press, 2006) and co-curator of the exhibition "The Downtown Show: The New York Art Scene, 1974–1984." The collection highlights and showcases some of the leading artworks and writings of the punk era and its founding origin in New York City and pays homage to a bygone era. Taylor is an expert on the details of this time period. He continues to do research in Victorian studies, experimental writing, English and American masculinities, downtown culture, contemporary art, and queer studies.

Marvin, tell us about yourself.

I'm a 60-year-old queer man who has been out since I was nineteen. Like most queers, I've played around with many narratives of style in my identity.

Early on, I did the whole plucked eyebrow thing with the most recent trendy fashions. Then I did the buttoned down look because I've been a professional rare book librarian. I've donned nice suits and handmade shirts. As a teenager and in my early days of college, I studied music classically, but also hung out with the punks and studio art kids.

I know you admire the punk genre of fashion. How do you feel that has reflected your personal identity?

I'm not sure I would call punk a genre of fashion. It was more about anti fashion when it started out, but it's certainly true that it's a personal self-styling that makes a statement about how the wearer views the world. There's a DIY, independent, hypercritical, snarky intellectuality behind the black leather, work boots, and haircuts of punks. There's also a complete rejection of hippies' unkemptness. The punk and new wave return to the styling and clothes of the early 1960s was a gesture toward a time when there was glamour that the hippies tried to destroy. This always appealed to me. As I grew older, I found myself more and more at home— and at work—in jeans, black work shoes or boots, and a black leather jacket. It's a kind of easy masculinity for me. It still includes nicely tailored black suits, black T-shirts (no ties anymore), and clunky, well-made black wingtips. I'm into the minimalness of it all … for me this wardrobe is a conscious decision.

Do you think that a gay fashion genre exists? Would you call it gay or queer?

I think there are people who want a "gay fashion genre" to exist and there are gay men who style themselves to match those expectations. I'm not always sure some of the men I meet know they are being forced into a marketing brand that is constructing their identity. That identity possibility is so strong in our culture that it may seem natural to them. When I was young, I felt the pressures of conforming to the "gay fashion genre," but it felt as uncomfortable to me as the word *gay*. The problem with the idea of a "gay fashion genre" is that it assumes certain commonalities among gay men that are created by the market and don't correspond to the diversity of queerness that's out there. I'm hesitant to talk about it as "queer fashion genre" lest I fall into a marketing genre for *queer*, which I want to use as a theoretical tool for looking at culture as well as a descriptor for how I live in the world.

Do gay men prefer certain fashion brands to others? And do gay men respond to brands that advertise toward their market?

Doesn't everyone? That's how the market works: it builds narratives that you can fit your identity into and sells them to you as natural, authentic, true. Of course, that's all crap, but it's how the system functions. I can only

(Continued)

speak for my circle of friends, but I notice that they follow the trends much more than I do. That said, I have brand loyalty to organizations that support queer rights and boycott those that do not. I'm also loyal to brands that make good products: Brooks Brothers, Red Wing, Church's Shoes.

Do you think the younger generations are more accepting of gay style and fashion? Do you think so-called straight men have adopted gay style over the years?

Straight men have always adopted gay fashion to some extent. Look at the Arrow Collar ads from the early part of the twentieth century. The male gaze at the male body—the homoerotic gaze—both fascinates and terrifies straight men. They see beautiful men in beautiful clothes and envy, emulate, and revolt at what they see. When gay men flaunted a more effeminate style, it was easy for straight men to reject gay fashion. These days, the gay code of "straight acting" has overshadowed the more flamboyant fun of earlier queer styles to the point that straight men feel comfortable with gay fashion. Of course, the great strides that queer politics have made in the past forty years also affect the changes we see. To put this all in perspective, however, many straight men wear black leather jackets and jeans, a look that grew out of the Chicago and southern California gay BDSM scenes in the 1940s and 50s. They don't know that history, but they enjoy the masculine look of it. I just wish they would adopt queer stylings sooner, such as the goatee, and let them go just as quickly.

Life Changes and Growth

That same year, Vivienne moved to Italy with her new business partner, Carlo d'Amario, and created a new collection called Hypnos (1984) at his home in the Alps. The collection featured garments made out of synthetic sports fabrics in bright fluorescent colors that fastened with buttons resembling a rubber phallus. It was selected and shown in Tokyo, along with Claude Montana, Gianfranco Ferre, and Calvin Klein, at the Hanae Mori's Best Five Western Designers Show. Hypnos was followed by the collection Clint Eastwood (1984–5), inspired by wide-open spaces with large silhouettes and the continuation of Day-Glo colors.[11]

In 1986, Vivienne returned to London and reopened her boutique World's End. She started new lines such as her Harris Tweed (1987) collection and continued to challenge herself in the area of design. She traveled and began teaching classes, becoming an Appointed Professor of Fashion at the Vienna Academy of Applied Arts in 1989. There she met her eventual husband, Andreas Kronthaler. In 1990, she was named the Designer of the Year at the British Fashion Council Awards.

Westwood's first complete menswear collection, called Cut and Slash, was completed in 1990 and was shown at the Pitti Uomo tradeshow in Florence. The first Vivienne Westwood shop opened at 6 Davies Street in London's Mayfair area and sold the Gold Label Collection. In 1991, Westwood's collection was shown at Tokyo's Fashion Summit along with Christian Lacroix, Isaac Mizrahi, and Franco Moschino. The year 1992 was very busy, as Westwood introduced a wedding gown into her runway collection shows and was made an Honorary Senior Fellow of the Royal College of Art. She continued opening shops, with a new location in London at 43 Conduit Street. Westwood also franchised her brand by designing a watch for Swatch called "Putti." That same year she was honored by Her Majesty Queen Elizabeth II and received an OBE (Order of the British Empire). She married Andreas Kronthaler, who is twenty-five years her junior.

In 1993, Westwood was Appointed Professor of Fashion at the Berliner Hochschule der Künste. She designed her second Swatch watch called "Orb," which became an instant collector's item. Westwood also designed and commissioned her own tartan plaid called the "Mac Andreas" for the Anglomania collection as a tribute to her husband. Westwood also moved into multichannel retailing when she designed a collection for the Littlewoods mail-order catalog in 1994; and that same year she won the first Institute of Contemporary Art Award for outstanding Contribution to Contemporary Culture. In 1996, Westwood's menswear line Man was launched in Milan, and she was featured in the three-part Channel 4 series *Painted Ladies*. As the company continued to grow internationally, in 1998 Vivienne Westwood Ltd was awarded the Queen's Award for Export. That same year, Westwood debuted her first fragrance, Boudoir. In 1999, her brand expanded as Westwood launched her new Red Label in the United States, coinciding with the opening of her first shop in New York City. Her accessory line was also introduced, which included eyewear as well as the Coquetteries body and bath line.

In 2000, the Museum of London held an exhibition honoring Vivienne Westwood. And during this same year, the second fragrance was launched, called Libertine. The first Moët & Chandon Fashion Tribute held in 2001 celebrated Vivienne Westwood as Designer of the Year. In 2002, Westwood opened her first shop in Hong Kong as well as an accessories shop. In 2003 she opened another store in Milan, and in 2004 the Victoria and Albert Museum featured a retrospective on the designer. In 2006, Vivienne Westwood was made a Dame in Queen Elizabeth's New Year's Honors list, and in 2007 Westwood was awarded the Outstanding Achievement in Fashion at the British Fashion Awards in London.

God Save the Planet: A Focus on Philanthropy

During the twenty-first century Westwood continued her antiestablishment, human rights, and sustainability mission. She demonstrated her commitment to it in 2010 with her International Trade Centre (United Nations) collaborations to create Ethical Fashion Initiatives in Kenya, producing handbags out of recycled materials.[12] In 2011, Westwood shot her ad campaign against the backdrop of Nairobi slums to draw attention to her Ethical Fashion Africa Program. Westwood has also designed for Chelsea Manning and for PETA, and she even cut off her hair in support of climate change action. In 2014, Westwood became the ambassador for the clean energy Trillion Fund.[13]

Also in 2011, Westwood joined forces with *Marie Claire International* and worked with them to produce a rainforest supplement that was printed in over twenty-seven editions of their magazines. She designed a T-shirt to coincide with the campaign in conjunction with the organization People Tree to raise money for indigenous tribes within the rainforest. Over the next year, she worked with organizations such as Cool Earth and Reprieve and unfolded a Climate Revolution banner at the 2012 Paralympics closing ceremony referencing her clothing collection of the same name. Westwood puts her money where her mouth is, and in 2012 she made a £1 million donation to rainforest charity Cool Earth. Her collections continued to represent her passion for sustainability with her Save the Arctic collection for autumn/winter 2013 and her Everything Is Connected collection, released for spring/summer 2014. On January 26, 2015, Westwood was seen outside the Houses of Parliament calling for Members of Parliament to vote for a moratorium on fracking within the United Kingdom (Figure 4.4).

Figure 4.4 English fashion designer and activist Vivienne Westwood addresses an antifracking rally outside the Houses of Parliament. (Photo by LEON NEAL/AFP via Getty Images)

Figure 4.5 Vivienne Westwood appears in public after a 16-week lockdown due to COVID-19 to protest about the illegal US extradition of Julian Assange for telling the truth about American war crimes. (Photo by Mike Marsland/WireImage)

In 2013, Vivienne Westwood utilized the importance of herself as a brand and through her philanthropic nature aided the English National Ballet.[14] In addition to her views on sustainability and supporting the arts, Westwood is a political activist. Her views impact the United Kingdom and are heard globally. On July 21, 2021, Dame Vivienne Westwood was suspended 10 feet high inside a giant bird cage in support of Julian Assange at the Old Bailey in London, England (Figure 4.5).

Street Style Success and Subcultural Leadership

There is probably no greater example of a successful designer using the ideas of the trickle-up theory (sometimes referred to as bubble-up) than Vivienne Westwood. Her street style sense and ability to turn it into haute couture was simply genius. According to the trickle-up theory, discussed in the works of both Dick Hebdige and George Sproles, fashion starts with the lower classes and then moves upwards as it is modified and recreated by the upper classes to wear.[15] The typical example of this is denim blue jeans, and how this garment moved from a gold rush miners' clothing garment made by Levi Strauss & Co. to mass fashion and eventually premium markets.

With Westwood, the brand/story of her success is the ability to capture the market through political protest and social issues recontextualizing into fashion apparel. For example, her T-shirts have continually challenged the status quo, with this author's personal favorite being Westwood's Cowboy T-shirt done for her "SEX" shop in 1975. These T-shirts have become so famous exhibitions have been mounted about them. In 1988, the T-shirts Westwood did for the famous band The Sex Pistols were exhibited at the New Museum for Contemporary Art in New York City (Figure 4.6).

With her success in fashion Westwood exemplifies the ideas of subcultural leadership. As George Sproles suggests, styles emerge from a lower socioeconomic group and are sometimes generated by rebellious youth such as the punks and hippies of the 1970s or the preppies of the 1980s. The youthfulness of these individuals plays a major role in the fashion shift and it becomes prestigious to the upper classes to mimic these fashions. In the case of Vivienne Westwood, her youthful punk fashion subcultural leadership became a fashion phenomenon in the world of design. In the simplest terms, Westwood impacted the fashion zeitgeist by making punk a high-end fashion trend

Figure 4.6 Malcolm McLaren (1946 –2010) center, in front of an installation of Sex Pistols ephemera, including T-shirts he designed with Vivienne Westwood, at the opening reception of his exhibition at the New Museum of Contemporary Art in New York City entitled "Impresario: Malcolm McLaren and the British New Wave" on September 14, 1988. (Photo by Catherine McGann/Getty Images)

and style that has become somewhat normalized. She is the queen of subcultural leadership in the punk style. This continues in her most recent collaboration, the March 2021 launch of her Asics sneakers, which reflect the ideology of her 1970s SEX collection, turning the sneaker into a punk-esque style.

What Will the Future Hold?

Vivienne Westwood stands for radicalism. She admires the unusual and is a major iconic designer who has built her reputation on not following the mainstream. Her success has been based on understanding and signifying those who are underrepresented, but by doing so she has shown those individuals who thought they were nonconformists that globally there are many similar individuals out there. She brings together all the outcasts of society by saying, "you are not alone." She is not afraid to make changes and do things a little differently by challenging cultural norms through political activism and social awareness. Dame Vivienne Westwood remains the rebel influence in fashion (Figure 4.7).

Figure 4.7 Vivienne Westwood on the runway at her London show during Fashion Week Men's collections on June 12, 2017. (Photo by Mike Marsland/Mike Marsland/WireImage)

Discussion Questions

1. How did Vivienne Westwood begin designing fashions? Can you describe the Vivienne Westwood brand?
2. What was the genre of music that Vivienne Westwood inspired? Give examples of some of the music bands she inspired and describe their looks. (You might have to do a little internet research.)
3. Do some research on the current names and divisions of the Vivienne Westwood brand. Can you name them all?
4. Later in life, Vivienne Westwood switched from a focus on fashion to a focus on what? What social or political organizations has she worked for in the last few years?

Expand Your Knowledge

Vivienne Westwood has been given the title of the godmother of punk music. She helped inspire and brand the British ideal of what punk music was all about. For this exercise, identify an iconic designer (you can include Vivienne Westwood) and discuss how he or she has inspired looks and style in the music industry. Can you think of any fashion designers that are in fact musicians? Write a short paper (two to three pages) about this topic.

Further Exploration

Watch:
I-D, *i-Cons: Vivienne Westwood* (2016), https://www.youtube.com/watch?v=ECZJE16uyPw (accessed April 25, 2021).
Read:
Vivienne Westwood and Ian Kelly, *Vivienne Westwood* (London: Picador, 2015).

Chapter 5
A Designer of Branded Occasions: Vera Wang

Chapter Objectives

> Review the brand/story of Vera Wang
> Discuss Vera Wang's impact on the figure skating community
> Consider how Vera Wang capitalized on the wedding market
> Reveal Vera Wang's transition from high-market fashion to mass merchandising

Figure 5.0 Vera Wang. (Photo by Marc Royce/Corbis via Getty Images)

In 1990 Vera Ellen Wang founded a design company reflecting her lifelong love of fashion and celebrating the romance, sensuality, and spirit of modern young women. She took the simple idea of designing her wedding dress and, in fewer than twenty years, turned it into a multimillion-dollar company that now includes a deluge of products and home accessories that reflect an elaborate lifestyle brand. The tremendous success of Vera Wang comes from her talent for creating storybook weddings and her practical experiences as a former *Vogue* editor and Ralph Lauren merchandiser. The latter role equipped her for creating a successful mass-marketed line of products called *Simply Vera*. Wang is an international design magnate whose products maintain a brand image of elegance, no matter where they are selling. Her career is a guide for all who study or want to work in fashion; the road to success has many twists and turns but maintaining focus and integrity will undoubtedly lead to triumph.

Vera Wang: Wedding Expert and Role Model

Vera Ellen Wang started her business in 1990 when she could not find a dress for her wedding ceremony. She designed one herself and since then has redefined the concept of wedding dresses and the entire ceremonial package. Wang designs and has licensing agreements for everything from couture wedding gowns to bridesmaid dresses, lingerie, china, stemware, flatware, barware, home décor, fine paper products, liquor, and fragrances, and Wang has even written a book. Not only does Wang provide the perfect wedding dress with all the accoutrements, but she can also supply a place for the wedding couple to sleep through a licensing agreement with Serta mattresses. In addition to making wedding-related products, Wang has joined the ranks of fashion designers who have branched out to big-box retailing with a mass-marketed line of reasonably priced clothing. Vera Wang's clear vision for her company continues to foster its growth.

Vera Wang is a role model for today's young fashionistas. Her career path reflects a woman who is educated, cultured, and able to transfer skills from one area of expertise to another. Because of retail consolidations, industry mergers, and changes in other fashion arenas, many who work in the fashion industry have to move from job to job. So although students of fashion, retailing, and merchandising sometimes expect to land their dream job as soon as they graduate from college, it might take some time to reach this goal. Vera Wang's story shows that while staying focused and pursuing one's ultimate career is essential, opportunities that may seem unrelated should not be neglected. One never knows where the fashion path will lead. Vera Wang's career has evolved from the focused business strategy of creating *the best* wedding dress to licensing agreements and a mass-merchandised lifestyle line of fashion for women throughout the United States. She has built a fashion empire; she is a role model for us all.

Who Is Vera Wang?

The intensity of focus that has made Vera Ellen Wang a success in the fashion world also led her to prosper in other areas. She was born in New York City on June 27, 1949 to an affluent family. Her father, Cheng-Ching Wang, had found success in Asia by creating distribution routes for pharmaceutical companies after the Second World War. He wanted Vera to pursue a career in medicine or law; he never dreamed of being a fashion designer. But Vera Wang had a passion for the arts and design.[1]

Until the age of nineteen, Vera Wang trained to be a figure skater. She competed in the 1968 US Figure Skating Championships and was a featured athlete in the January 8, 1968 issue of *Sports Illustrated*. Her love of fashion began with the designs for her skating costumes. She also visited high-end designer showrooms and runway shows with her mother, Florence Wang, and brother, Kenneth Wang. Vera's primary goal was to be an Olympic skater, but unfortunately, she did not make the team.[2]

Vera Wang attended the Chapin School in Manhattan and then enrolled at Sarah Lawrence College. She spent some time at the Sorbonne in Paris, where she discovered her love of design. After her sophomore year at college, Vera gave up her figure-skating career and pursued her interest in fashion and design.[3]

While in college, Wang worked as a sales associate at Yves Saint Laurent. One of her clients, Frances Stein, an editor at *Vogue*, befriended Wang and encouraged her to apply at *Vogue* once she graduated. Wang did just that, and after college, she acquired a position at *Vogue* magazine. At age twenty-one, she was hired as a rover, or temporary assistant, for editor Polly Mellen. Wang did whatever they asked her to do, such as sweeping floors, providing yogurt for models, and getting coffee. She was a glorified gofer. But she knew her enthusiasm and work ethic would pay off.

At the age of twenty-three, Wang became the youngest editor *Vogue* had ever employed. During her sixteen years at *Vogue*, Wang attained senior editor and design director's title for accessories.[4] She took a leave of absence from *Vogue* after interviewing for editor-in-chief, the position that Anna Wintour currently holds. At age thirty-four, Wang returned to Paris for two years and spent time decorating her apartment. When she returned from Paris, she resigned from her post at *Vogue*.

Wang transferred her experience as senior editor at the most popular women's magazine to begin her design career. With her networking skills and contacts from *Vogue*, she was able to tackle the position of design director for Ralph Lauren accessories.[5] It was at Lauren that Wang discovered her interest in mass fashion design. She was able to transfer her research skills in accessories to design. She brought with her extensive knowledge of the women's accessories market and the current leading brands and expertise in fashion forecasting and merchandising.

Vera Wang's Branding Story

Vera Wang's branding story began in 1989 when she and Arthur Becker planned their wedding. After all her years in top-level jobs in the fashion industry, it was through the search for the perfect wedding dress that Wang found her calling. She wanted a dress that was contemporary and reflective of current styles. She found the dresses in the target market too dowdy, not in good taste, or just plain ordinary, which forced her to design her own dress. Now be mindful, Vera Wang does not consider herself a "bridal designer"; instead, she is a designer who happens to create wedding dresses. This thought process allows her to think "outside the box" when creating new looks for brides and not be stagnated by the ideals of strict bridal design.

The following year, she opened her luxury salon in the Carlyle Hotel in New York, which featured a line of fashionable wedding dresses. The original boutique started a trend in modern wedding gown styles. Wang began to introduce gowns at various price points representing "good, better, and best." For example, a good Vera Wang dress can cost between $3,000 and $7,000, the Vera Wang Luxe Collection is priced from about $6,000 to $20,000, and a Vera Wang couture gown runs much more. A couture customer bride usually consults with a chief designer and might even meet Vera Wang herself.

The Vera Wang style became the epitome of wedding fashion, worn by numerous celebrities. An example is the dress designed for Jennifer Lopez when she married Marc Anthony in 2004. Other famous brides have included Jessica Simpson, Thalia, Avril Lavigne, Victoria Beckham, Jennifer Garner, Campbell Brown, Jeri Ryan, Uma Thurman, Mariah Carey, and Karenna Gore. And Vera Wang even designed a wedding dress for the most popular woman in popular culture—Barbie (Figure 5.1).

Figure 5.1 A Mattel Barbie doll dressed by fashion designer Vera Wang stands for sale at a toy store in New York, February 3, 2009. (Photo by Emmanuel Dunand/AFP via Getty Images)

Vera Wang was introduced to Hollywood through Sharon Stone when Stone wore a Vera Wang sarong on the red carpet. They continued to build their friendship and attended many events together. Holly Hunter wore a Vera Wang original when she won the Oscar for *The Piano*, and Jane Fonda was outfitted and styled by Vera Wang when she re-entered the scene after her divorce from Ted Turner. Charlize Theron made her first debut on the red carpet in a stunning Vera Wang halter gown. Theron was placed on the best-dressed lists that year.

A Short Brand/Story	Fashioning Personal Brand Success: Interview with Amanda Buchanan

As a senior recruiter for IKEA group, Amanda Buchanan works to ensure effective hiring practices for leadership positions within IKEA stores throughout the East Coast of the United States. As part of IKEA's recruitment leadership team, Amanda is committed to shaping a high-performance team that leverages diversity, equity, and inclusion best practices.

With over fifteen years of solid and progressive experience in human resources, retail, and diversity, equity and inclusion, Amanda has held a wide range of responsibilities in both field and staff functions. Before entering

(Continued)

the world of recruitment, she served as a case manager for KRA Corporation, diversity specialist at Cigna Corporation, and held the role of Executive Team Leader of Human Resources at Target. Her academic, corporate, and field experiences provide her with a unique skillset enabling a diverse career as both teacher and recruiter.

Amanda has served as a board member of the Philadelphia Chapter of the National Black MBA Association. She is an active member of the Urban League of Philadelphia's Extraordinary Talent Network (NExT Philadelphia).

Amanda received her Bachelor of Business Administration in International Business and a Bachelor of Arts in Spanish from Loyola University Maryland. She later went on to receive her Master of Business Administration from Villanova University. Amanda resides in Delaware County with her husband and two-year-old daughter. She loves to travel, participate in community outreach activities, DIY projects, and running.

What do you look for in a potential job candidate as regards their personal brand?

As a recruiter, the things I look for first and foremost are ENERGY and PASSION! As a retail recruiter, I'm constantly looking for individuals who are naturally enthusiastic about their work because they will need to bring that to work every day—working with various personality types and having the wherewithal to work under pressure. These are all qualities that make up the personal brand of individuals who will thrive in retail and fashion careers. Your brand is what makes you, YOU! It's the perception you give others. Research estimations state the average person in the US is exposed to at least five thousand brands daily. We live in a world full of brands, which is why we need to understand the importance of branding, not just how it applies to products and businesses, but how it applies to us as individuals.

What career tips would you offer a young professional looking to grow in the area of fashion and retailing?

I want young professionals to know that it's okay to try new things! The path to greatness is not always straight up the ladder! Sometimes you have to take lateral moves, and other times you must step down to step up. No matter where you are in your career, take it as an opportunity to learn all you can because these are the skills you will use to build on your career.

While a good appearance is vital for a candidate, are soft skills just as essential?

Soft skills are critical to your success! Being an effective communicator, showing empathy, having integrity and accountability, and resilience and adaptability are things that I look for daily! So many people can do a job, but can they bring these skills that are so necessary to run the business while putting people first? These are skills that we can't constantly develop in the workplace, but we can help people hone in on these areas and enhance them through their work experience.

Where do you see future careers in fashion and retailing? What does the future fashion professional look like?

While we see more companies leaning on their e-commerce business, I believe we will see retailers create more "Experiences" in the future. Whether through enhanced stores that feature wow factors that bring people in or via pop-up installations where people can experience products in unique ways, retail business will always remain relevant, although it may change its form. The future fashion or retail professional is ever evolving, adaptable to the evolving times and processes, and able to think with their target customer in mind.

Wang Builds Her Brand Name

In addition to the dresses, Wang's clients started to ask her to plan their weddings or to recommend certain types of accoutrements for the event. So, she started designing nonclothing items, among other things. These became licensed businesses for Vera Wang; her china and crystal are manufactured by Waterford Wedgwood and her silver plates and glasses by Syratech. Her book titled *Vera Wang on Weddings* (HarperCollins, 2002) provides specifics for the ultimate wedding.

Wang also designed a line of fragrances as part of the Vera Wang branding image. They include Vera Wang, Sheer Veil, Princess, and Vera Wang for Men. All the fragrances are licensed through an exclusive deal with Coty. As with many high-end designer lines, mass-produced fragrances allow mass customers to own a piece of Vera Wang's product line because many are priced at less than $100. These mass-produced international fragrances have sold in vast quantities. With an expanded business strategy and extra funds gained from fragrance sales and licensing agreements with Waterford Wedgewood, Syratech, and Coty, Wang has been able to maintain the integrity of her wedding gowns while moving into other clothing lines.

Throughout her career, Wang has maintained her passion for figure skating, designing costumes for figure skaters, including Nancy Kerrigan and Michelle Kwan. Kerrigan helped build Wang's brand by winning the 1994 Olympic Games while wearing a Vera Wang original. This white dress was modeled on the dress Marilyn Monroe wore when she sang "Happy Birthday" to President John F. Kennedy. But Vera did not just design skating dresses for figure skaters; in 2009 she dressed the Olympic champion figure skater Kristi Yamaguchi (Figure 5.2) on her way to an event at Bryant Park in New York City.

The figure-skating community has never forgotten the contributions that Vera Wang has made to their community. They respect her so

Figure 5.2 Figure skater Kristi Yamaguchi wears a Vera Wang dress in Bryant Park, New York City on February 13, 2009. (Photo by Ray Tamarra/Getty Images)

Figure 5.3 Designer Vera Wang is inducted into the US Figure Skating Hall of Fame during the AT&T US Figure Skating Championships at Quicken Loans Arena, Cleveland, Ohio on January 23, 2009. (Photo by Matthew Stockman/Getty Images)

Figure 5.4 Models pose during the Australian showcase of Vera Wang Brides Spring 2017 Collection on September 14, 2016 in Sydney, Australia. (Photo by Don Arnold/WireImage)

much, that on January 23, 2009, Wang was inducted into the US Figure Skating Hall of Fame during the AT&T US Figure Skating Championships at Quicken Loans Arena (Figure 5.3). This was a tremendous honor for Wang, who had given up skating for fashion design, but had truly never forgotten how much she loved the sport.

In 2005, when the upscale department store Bergdorf Goodman installed a Vera Wang salon on the third floor of its flagship store on Fifth Avenue, Vera Wang had genuinely arrived in women's fashion. That same year, the Council of Fashion Designers of America named Vera Wang the Year's Womenswear Designer. Her retail success has gone global, with flagship stores expanding from New York to Sydney, Australia. Each boutique remains focused on making quality gowns and products. Wang's bridal designs are globally accepted as leading in this category and she continues to reinvent the vision and look of bridal design (Figure 5.4).

Vera Wang's Mass Merchandising

With success in the high-end and luxury markets, Vera Wang shifted direction to mass public consumption to increase sales beyond an annual $15 million. In the fall of 2005, Vera Wang launched new fine jewelry and luxe lingerie lines that brought almost $300 million in retail store sales. This success proved that the company had potential in the mass market. However, even these products were geared toward an upper-middle-class, affluent clientele. The company was not reaching larger audiences and gaining its dollar share of the mass market.

Wang began to think that her name needed to reach more than just a few high-end department store consumers who were buying her lines. She realized that the expensive goods she was designing would not allow everyone to have Vera Wang. In her words, "few women really can afford a $2,000 dress, so I would love to design clothing that people can actually afford."[6]

On Sunday, September 9, 2007, Vera Wang launched her Simply Vera product line at Kohl's department stores at 749 locations nationwide. Through a long-term licensing agreement with the Menomonee, Wisconsin retailer, this collection featured sportswear, intimate apparel, handbags, leather accessories, jewelry, footwear, bed linens, and towels.[7] The line's price points reflect a very moderate range, with dresses from $70 to $100 and other products at prices similar to those found at retailers such as Banana Republic. The clothing is extremely well designed, size inclusive, and the fashionable style reflects the Vera Wang brand. She states it best:

> For me, Simply Vera, Vera Wang represents not just a fashion philosophy, but a vision about life and style. It's also a true expression of my own personal design vocabulary … the deliberate mixing and matching of different weights, colors, and textures … layering for charm, style, and comfort … relaxed shapes and silhouettes with subtle artistic flourishes. I also love an element of surprise here and there, a touch of the unexpected. Details on a dress can inspire bed linens, and jewelry or embellishments can adorn a bag or a shoe. This juxtaposition of ideas speaks to a modern sensibility that is fun, easy, and sophisticated. Casual can be stylish, dressy can be casual. From the runway to the red carpet, the aisle to the home, my hope is that Simply Vera, Vera Wang gives women the confidence to express their own personal style.[8]

The Simply Vera line has gone global and sells in various retail outlets worldwide, such as at Harris Scarfe in Australia. Simply Vera has taken Kohl's to another level of consumer and has allowed company growth in such areas as New York City. Kohl's has done pop-up opening events for Simply Vera in Manhattan (Figure 5.5) with Wang herself as the guest

Figure 5.5 Vera Wang kicks off the holiday season with Kohl's in New York City at their "New Gifts At Every Turn" pop-up on November 6, 2019. (Photo by Jennifer Graylock/Getty Images for Kohl's)

star. They have been successful at creating a spectacular brand/story and public relations image for Vera Wang herself.

Her success in mass merchandising with Kohl's was so popular that she saw hope in another mass market retail venture. So, in 2011, Vera Wang launched her licensed White collection for David's Bridal, allowing those brides who may not be able to afford the higher-priced Vera Wang dresses to buy one through the David's Bridal retail outlets. The line has been very successful and continues to grow into one of the company's leading lifestyle lines. At an event on January 11, 2019, Wang stated that the line reflects her ideas of a wedding dress, "It's not just another dress. It's the dress that you'll remember forever" (Figure 5.6).

Vera Wang has many leading branding partners that ensure that the line maintains its integrity. It is dedicated to designs that reflect the true Vera Wang style—sophistication, simplicity, and perfection. The company has over two hundred employees in US manufacturing and tailoring who create the bridal gown collection. The detailing required to make these gowns is labor intensive, but the company maintains a high production level by hiring the best designers and tailors. As a student who worked

Figure 5.6 Mannequins during An Evening with Vera Wang presented by Brides and David's Bridal on January 11, 2019 in New York City. (Photo by Cindy Ord/Getty Images for WHITE by Vera Wang)

for Vera Wang said, "Everyone is treated very well. Vera is great, and she demonstrates hard work with humility. She is very professional and gives wonderful feedback. When you work for Vera Wang, you know that you are respected for your talents and skills."[9]

The Career Continues

Fashion is Vera Wang's passion. She has dedicated her life to becoming a leader in the industry and is an excellent role model for anyone aspiring to succeed in business. She has proven that you can pursue your dreams and reach your ultimate goal. Although many critics have stated that Wang had it easy because of her father's money, she would not have attained this level of success without her passion, focus, and drive. Vera Wang works hard and is loyal to her brand. The company continues to grow and may well be on the way to becoming a global brand. With products that range from couture fashions to bed linens, the future looks bright for Vera Wang's empire.

Discussion Questions

1. In what way is Vera Wang a great example of the ever-changing career path of an individual?
2. Go to www.verawang.com. What changes have occurred in the company since the writing of this chapter? Has the brand expanded into other products?
3. In your own words, describe the Vera Wang brand. How does this brand differ from others, such as Ralph Lauren or Vivienne Westwood?

Expand Your Knowledge

It is time for some self-reflection by answering the following questions: What are your professional plans for the future? How do you intend to make those plans happen? What stumbling blocks do you think you will have to clear along the way? How long do you think it will take to reach your goals? Next, do a theoretical charting of your career from now until age fifty, and make sure you examine each position. If you don't know the names of certain professions, research them. What are your financial goals, your personal goals? Can you do it all? Discuss all your thoughts in class.

Further Exploration

Watch:
Oxford Union, *Vera Wang Oxford Union* (2018), https://www.youtube.com/
    watch?v=p13cf96arvo (accessed April 25, 2021).
Read:
Vera Wang, *Vera Wang on Weddings* (New York: Harper Design, 2001).

GAP

Chapter 6
The Branding of Masstige: The Gap, Inc.

Chapter Objectives

> Understand the conceptualization of masstige branding using Gap
> Give a brief history of Gap
> Discuss the impact of Gap's branding campaigns and how they changed fashion
> Reveal how Gap impacts social diversity, equity, and inclusion through media merchandising and continues this vision

Figure 6.0 Betty Boo for the Individuals of Style Campaign, 1990. (Photo courtesy of Advertising Archives)

It seems The Gap, Inc. has been forgotten, almost swallowed up by the H&Ms, Zaras, and Uniqlos of the world. But what is important to remember is that it was Gap that started it all with fast fashion. The company is over fifty years old and was the first to take the private label, contextualize it into fantastic advertising campaigns, and make ordinary everyday clothes masstige. By combining their brand of clothing in advertising with the likes of celebrities like Betty Boo (Figure 6.0) the company gave their garments a reputation for quality and style, as you will see in this chapter. Yes, Gap did borrow from Ralph Lauren and Lacoste, taking standard style icons like the polo shirt and turning them into mass fashion, but Gap did it differently. It merchandised its line of simplistic, logo-free apparel goods with other designer brands, celebrities, and even fashion designers so that its products were associated with high style. It introduced the famous Gap hoodie and revolutionized the idea that you do not have to spend a lot of money to buy a quality garment. And it did so in a democratized manner, demonstrating support for social and cultural issues such as gay rights, anti-agism, and racial and gender equality in its branding campaigns.

Gap held tight to the San Bruno, California values of letting each person's individual style celebrate who they are and who they want to be; they even named a campaign "Individuals of Style" after it and change the way we look at fashion today.

With its mission to sell essential clothing with a twist of fashion flair, the company has had its share of ups and downs. Gap's fortunes are similar to the fashion bell curve, going in and out of vogue. Gap now operates Banana Republic, Old Navy, Intermix, Athleta, and the upcoming Yeezy Gap. It is the largest specialty retailer in the United States. It has the third most international locations among mass fashion retailers behind Inditex Group and H&M. Gap has outlet stores with a Gap Factory and Banana Republic Factory store. These stores offer a different assortment of products than the traditional retail locations. The company has approximately 3,500 retail locations located in North America, Europe, Asia, the Middle East, South America, and Africa (company-owned and franchised).[1] The company's products and services are available through the online website Gap.com. Gap also utilizes third parties that provide logistical assistance and fulfillment centers. Gap uses an omni-channel approach to retailing, connecting the digital world to its actual brick-and-mortar locations. The company tries to enhance the buying experience by reflecting specific social and cultural events. The COVID-19 pandemic allowed the store to grow in website orders, curbside pick-up, order-in-store, find-in-store, and ship-from-store. They have enhanced all mobile experiences tailored to each brand and division.[2] The company also uses "Gap Inc. Insiders," an online community that encourages customer feedback by awarding gift cards and discounts. Customers must fill out a survey to become part of the group as they are accepted, based upon specific demographics.

Gap continues to reach new audiences through branding campaigns and its ability to tell good stories. So come along as we "Fall into The Gap" and read about this retailing giant and its impact on baby boomer, gen X, millennial, and gen Z's mass fashion style. The Gap is one retailer responsible for moving us from the traditional four fashion seasons of fall, winter, spring, and summer into almost a new season every month. This retailer and innovative brand has influenced fashion forever.

Gap History and the Sweat Wall

Gap was founded in 1969 by Donald and Doris F. Fisher with the simple idea of providing jeans with an easier fit. By the third year in business, the company had opened over twenty-five stores, and by 1974 Gap private-label merchandise has become a part of their fashion assortment. In 1976, Gap went public, and by 1977 the company had launched two new stores, Logo, which catered to a more mature shopper and Brands, which offered a value-priced garment; neither is now in existence. In 1978, Gap introduced "Gap Fashion Pioneers," their brand of jeans and corduroy pants.[3]

By the early 1980s Gap stores had grown so much in popularity that the company introduced the SuperGap. In 1983, the company purchased Banana Republic, which had two stores and a catalog business.[4] The store was known as the Banana Republic: Travel & Safari Clothing Company, with stores representing a safari excursion selling functional garments, almost like an army surplus store (Figure 6.1). The company would own another brand in the 1980s called Hemisphere, which was to become their luxury label, but soon closed these stores and puts its efforts into

Figure 6.1 Banana Republic: Travel & Safari Clothing Company store in Manhattan, New York City. (Photo by Bob Krist)

Banana Republic. It would be years for Banana Republic became what it is today, but this division still celebrates its original roots through its line of clothing called Heritage.

During the 1980s, Gap would begin focusing on their primary garment lines to build volume. These included polo shirts, T-shirts, shaker knit sweaters, Henley tops, sweatshirts, sweatpants, ball caps, and socks. Creating their private labels, Gap developed brands such as Work Force denim (Figure 6.2), allowing for higher profit margins. The company used the famous brand advertising photographer Herb Ritts. This new method of telling stories about their Gap products stylized through high-end black and white photography gained them new customers, competing with designers such as Ralph Lauren. This was at the time when Ralph Lauren was having Bruce Weber create lifestyle merchandising photo layouts for him (Chapter 3) and when this type of advertising was gaining success and popularity for many fashion labels.

If anyone shopped or worked for Gap during the mid-1980s, they remember the "sweat wall." During this time, the company would become known for sweats, in addition to its jeans. Using print advertising in magazines to promote their basic lines of sweatshirts

WORK FORCE

Denim—it's the stuff dreams are made of.
Dreams of cowboys and builders, of dancers and writers,
of men with broad shoulders and women with long legs. It is
part of the fabric of American life, the clothes we go to work in
and have a good time in. Clothing you'll want to live in
day after day and night after night.

Figure 6.2 An early Gap brand was Work Force, photographed by Herb Ritts; these ads gave Gap a new image. (Photo courtesy of Advertising Archives)

and sweatpants, Gap centered the back of their stores on these products. The sweat wall was an homage to rows of colors of sweatshirts and sweatpants. The back of each store looked like giant vertical stripes of color. The wall would be merchandised throughout the season with new colors and styles.

No longer were Champion and Russell the only sweat garment companies; Gap wanted a piece of this fashion market, and they got it. The placement of sweats on the center-back wall enticed customers to walk through Gap stores, perhaps stopping at other clothing racks. The process was genius for gaining units per transaction and building average sales.

Gap eventually became iconic for one of their sweatshirt creations, the Gap logo zip-front hooded sweatshirt. This company garment eventually became the garment copied by other mass fashion retail companies and top designers, but Gap did it first! In 2018, its iconic sweatshirt was featured in an article titled "GQ for Gap 2018: The Iconic Sweatshirt, Reimagined." *GQ* and Gap asked famous designers what their vision would be for the renowned sweatshirt moving forward. While many think Gap is synonymous with jeans, the company has also built a reputation around being a go-to for sweat gear! So much so that even today, customers return four if not five times a year to purchase new colors (Figure 6.3).

Figure 6.3 The colorful women's sweat wall of the Gap Factory Outlet Store, Winter 2021–22. (Photo by author)

New Fashion Gatekeeping: Individuals of Style and Everyone in Khaki

Gap continued to build its popularity, featuring their product prominently on actors in films, such as Michael J. Fox in *Back To The Future* (1985, Universal Studios). Fox is spotted wearing a Gap pocket T. In 1986, Gap opened its first GapKids store, and in 1987, the company opened a store in London. The iconic Gap blue square logo gained popularity and became the company's official logo, and, by 1989, the Gap was opening stores in Canada.[5]

But the late 1980s saw the dawn of Gap becoming more than just store openings and new divisions. Gap took a twist when it became a mass fashion and cultural gatekeeper. The Gap's chief marketing officer, Maggie Gross, had an idea. Her vision was to put famous people in Gap pocket T's, Gap jean jackets, Gap denim jeans, and other basic garments, mixing and matching their looks with other renowned designer brands. Her vision included all these stars being photographed in black and white and stylized uniquely. She called the campaign "Individuals of Style," and it was a huge success, winning Gross an award in 1991.[6] This campaign reflected the times with key established celebrities as well as newcomers rising to fame. The campaign reflected social, cultural, and artistic movements. Gap became what the theorist Jean Hamilton (see Chapter 2) would call *arbiters of fashion* or what the industry dubs gatekeepers.[7]

Gap gained momentum and became an influence on the fashion industry across the globe, featuring stars such as the British-Malaysian singer Betty Boo (aka Allison Clark) (Figure 6.0), who had just launched her new CD *Boomania* (1990). In all the campaign photos, the celebrity wears one garment from Gap. For Clark, it is a Gap tank top. The ad allowed the viewer to see a star like Betty Boo incorporating Gap into her wardrobe. The ad gives customers fashion tips, and at the same time, Individuals of Style was free branding for the star, in this case, Betty Boo. It was the precursor to Facebook, TikTok, or Instagram, demonstrating how cool it is to wear Gap clothing as part of your style. Posters of celebrities such as Betty Boo hung in store windows across the United States and the United Kingdom. Many of the ads were known features in magazines such as *GQ* and *Vogue*.

With the success of the Individuals of Style campaign, Gap was all the rage! Gap stepped into the fashion spotlight on the April 1992 cover of *Vogue* with supermodels wearing Gap white denim jeans and woven shirts. This fashion cover made the company brand chic and the ideology of masstige fashion *something that everyone should have and could afford*! The success of Individuals of Style gave way to a new advertising campaign.[8]

In 1993, the company launched its "Who Wore Khakis" campaign featuring the likes of cultural icons Marilyn Monroe, Ernest Hemingway, Miles Davis (Figure 6.4), Zsa Zsa Gabor, and Gene Kelly, as well as other stars of yesteryear. The campaign created a flavor of nostalgia for a favorite garment—khaki pants. Even more incredible, this campaign did not feature Gap clothing! None of the ads displayed the celebrities wearing new Gap styles. Instead, many of the images were from decades gone by when Gap did not exist. Rather, saying "Miles Davis wore khakis," for example, allowed the company to associate with the celebrity and give a nostalgic feel, suggesting that Gap carried similar clothing or heritage basics.

But some found the campaign disturbing because of the fact that many of the celebrities, like Miles Davis, had passed away. Gap appeared to be profiting from the deceased. An article in *The Washington Post* by Christopher Corbett, "Ever-Chic Khaki and the Profitable Fascists," reported the negative overtones of khaki pants that Gap seemed to forget. According to Corbett, Benito Mussolini, Adolf Hitler, and Martin Bormann wore khakis

Figure 6.4 The Gap advertisement for Miles Davis wore khakis, 1993. (Photo courtesy of Advertising Archives)

too. The backlash was not well received by the public, who found the article offensive, and in the end, Gap was still on top.[9]

In 1996, another tie to celebrity culture played out to Gap's advantage as actress Sharon Stone wore a Valentino skirt, velvet Armani jacket, and a Gap black mock turtleneck for $26 during the Academy Awards. When asked what she is wearing, Stone answered, "I am wearing Gap … Swear to God!" The next day that mock turtleneck sold out, and is one of the most noted outfits today that was worn on the red carpet.[10] As the 1990s came to an end, Gap was no longer in the spotlight for Gap Inc. Instead, it was Old Navy and ads featuring the late Carrie Donovan (former editor for *Vogue*, *Harper's Bazaar*, and *The New York Times Magazine*) along with Magic the Dog that stole the limelight. However, Gap did make some home runs with their hit commercials featuring dancers performing such numbers as Gap Khaki's Swing, Mambo, and Gap Soul.[11]

A Short Brand/Story

Branding Mass Fashion and Off-Price Retail: Interview with Nancy Mair

In the world of fast fashion, stores such as Target, Gap, American Eagle, Primark, H&M, Uniqlo, Forever 21, and Old Navy usually take the spotlight. Sometimes left in the back of a young consumer's mind are retailers like TJ Maxx, Marshalls, Home Goods, and Ross stores.

Never thought of a career in the exciting world of off-price retail? Nancy Mair is the Global Off-Price Advisor for Empresas La Polar, the fourth-largest department store in Chile. She is also the President of NCM Consulting, retail consultants for million-dollar businesses. Nancy is a former Senior Vice President and General Merchandising Manager of Burlington Stores and is an alum of Drexel University. Nancy worked at Burlington for over twenty-six years, beginning as an intern and working her way up through the organization. She has led many teams of fifty people or more, responsible for more than $1 billion in annual sales. She was part of the executive team that strategized Burlington's turnaround and explosive growth after Bain Capital acquired the company in 2006. She left Burlington in 2018, starting her own consulting company, providing private equity, retailers, and wholesalers with knowledge and understanding to evolve their current businesses to be successful in the off-price model.

Please tell us about yourself and your career. Where did you grow up, go to school, work, etc.?

I grew up in Central Jersey, had my very first paying job as a retail associate at Annie Sez. I always enjoyed merchandising the fixtures, taking great pride in sizing and colorizing racks to make it easy for the customer to find what he or she is looking for. Yet, I grew up always knowing that I would follow my dream of being a nutritionist, authoring a successful diet book that would sell millions of copies. This dream took me to Drexel University, known for having an excellent Nutrition program. The first day, I met my college roommate, who proceeded to tell me she was a Fashion Design & Merchandising major. I didn't know universities offered a curriculum in that field, and after I heard what it entailed, I knew this was what I wanted to do! I had the passion for fashion, math and analyzing data, thinking on my feet, and creating strategies for building the perfect assortments for what customers would want. I changed my major my very first day, angering my father like I have never done before. I had two Co-ops while at Drexel, the second one working as an assistant buyer at Burlington Coat Factory, where I was hired right after graduation. I stayed at Burlington for twenty-six years, working my way up to Senior Vice President and General Merchandise Manager, leading teams of more than fifty people. Now, I consult for retailers, wholesalers, and manufacturers, helping them understand the off-price model and bring the concept to their company.

How is off-price retail different from other types of retail? Would you say your job is like that of the typical buyer or merchandiser?

Off-price is very different from other types of retail in a few ways. First of all, one of the most important aspects of off-price retailers is providing an exciting treasure hunt for the customer. Because we don't plan 100 percent of our open to buy, we always leave a large amount of liquidity each month for exciting deals. This makes the "rack" or "fixture" look different every time a customer comes into the store. You may find brands in off-price stores consistently, or you are likely to find something new and different, at prices much lower than other stores. Secondly, having the liquidity allows a merchant or a planner to shift open to buy dollars to categories that are selling. Department and specialty store buyers buy merchandise six to twelve months out and need to fill a fixture or planogram. Off-pricers aren't beholden that far in the future, nor is it important to fill a fixture. We are trained to "chase" trending businesses immediately and can cut back funds for businesses that are lagging. Lastly, off-price merchants focus on the retail value of the item they are buying, not what it costs. Focusing on what a customer should pay based on the competition within the rack or in another retailer is crucial for success.

How would you say that off-price is different from, say, Macy's? Is fashion branding harder to do in the off-price world of retail?

Off-price retailers carry the same name brands as department stores, but our customers don't have to wait for a sale or coupon to get great value. Customers can shop every day and know that the prices are the lowest every single day. Deliveries of new products arrive daily, so there is a reason to shop all the time. Because the prices are outstanding, product moves pretty quickly, so you need to buy it when you see it or it will be gone! As I mentioned before, department stores buy goods far in advance and can't react quickly to what the customer wants. Additionally, they buy a lot of depth in product, so you know you can go back to the store in a few weeks and it will most likely still be there. We can learn what the customer wants, go find it immediately in the market that week, and deliver it quickly so we are providing her with exactly what she wants, when she wants it. Off-price is where the customer wants to shop because we deliver everyday value. We focus on offering the right price the first moment it hits the floor, not counting on markdowns/coupons to drive our sales. The vendor community understands how important this part of retail is, so building partnerships with the right people is key.

What would your recommendations be to someone who wants to work in off-price retail or get a job working in your field?

If someone wants to work in off-price, my recommendation would be to competitively shop all aspects of retail. Learn about values in specialty stores, online, department stores, off-price, everywhere. Learn to be a student of all retail to understand delivering great value. Ask a ton of questions and use what you have learned to make decisions based on the situation at hand. A person must have passion and enthusiasm, be very creative and smart, think on his or her feet, as well as have an understanding that this business is ever changing. This person must learn guardrails of the business but gets that the business is always moving with the customer's choices and that person has to change just as quickly.

Into the Twenty-First-Century Groove

During the early twenty-first century, Gap expanded Old Navy to Canada and opened an outlet division. Donald Fisher, the founder of the company, stepped down in 2004, and in 2005 Banana Republic opened its doors in Japan. Advertising for the company continued to grow through television commercials that associated Gap with both celebrity and diversity. One of the company's most robust ads during this time was a remix of Madonna's *Into the Groove* and changing it to *Into the Hollywood Groove* featuring the star herself with Missy Elliott (Figure 6.5). The commercial promoted blue jeans and corduroys and was a huge success. Again, it was building on star power and the ideas of taking the garments to a whole new level with the celebrity style of

Figure 6.5 Still from the Madonna and Missy Elliott Gap commercial, "Into the Hollywood Groove," 2004. (Photo by The Gap via Getty Images)

Madonna and Missy Elliott. Both women were unique, stood out, and were different shapes and sizes; Gap was showing its consumers that they supported all women.[12]

In 2007 Gap developed its philanthropic efforts by partnering with PACE or the Personal Advanced Career Enhancement program, helping women who worked in Gap garment factories with life and work skills. But it was in 2006 when Gap again hit the fashion zeitgeist when it collaborated with Bono (lead singer of U2) and Bobby Shriver, releasing a line of products with half of the proceeds fighting HIV (AIDS) programs in Africa. Celebrities such as Penelope Cruz, the Spanish actress, are featured wearing Gap apparel along with their unique (Product)RED sayings such as DESI(RED) (Figure 6.6). The campaign was a success, bringing Gap into the fashion spotlight across the globe to support philanthropy. The brand built upon the use of celebrities to heighten its product quality and status. In 2008, Gap acquired Athleta activewear and had opened stores by 2011.

In November 2010, the Gap opened a new flagship store in Beijing, China, and featured a special edition of their 1969 denim blue jeans (Figure 6.7). This store was a significant step in expanding the Gap

Figure 6.6 A Gap billboard on Mission Street, San Francisco, California, November 2, 2006. (Photo by David Paul Morris/Getty Images)

Figure 6.7 A Chinese worker holds a pair of jeans at clothing retailer Gap's newly-opened flagship store in Beijing on November 15, 2010. (Photo courtesy of STR/AFP via Getty Images)

brand, which was aiming at doubling the company revenue outside the United States. Consumers flooded into the Gap stores to purchase the special edition apparel featuring special packaging.

Labor Controversy and Change

Gap has not always been seen in a positive light. From 1999 to 2007, the company faced allegations of sweatshop labor, forcing employees to work up to 109 hours per week, with some not being paid for six months, and child labor practices in Indian Gap factories. In all cases, the company addressed the allegations, enhancing production technology and compensation for the workers in those countries, using fair wage labor practices outlined by US law. Even in their home country, Gap was scrutinized over low compensation, but on February 19, 2014, the then CEO Glenn Murphy announced it would raise the wages of its 65,000 employees.[13] Gap also took steps in the right direction by partnering with Bangladesh Worker Safety to improve factory conditions in all their Bangladesh factories.[14]

With their new positive drive towards global work equality, then-President Barack Obama made a stop in the Manhattan Gap store to show his support for the iconic retailer (Figure 6.8). This visit represented the

Figure 6.8 US President Barack Obama shops for clothing for his family alongside store employee Susan Panariello during a visit to a Gap clothing store in New York City. (Photo courtesy of Saul Loeb/AFP via Getty Images)

President's support for raising the minimum wage for all US employees and showed his care and concerns for retail workers. This political move put Gap in the spotlight as a national treasure.

Moving Forward

In 2017, Gap opened new stores in New York's Times Square, showcasing their unique look and feel. The company relaunched its 1990s archive in stores that same year. In 2018, Gap launched a men's high-level performance-wear brand Hill City. However, it closed the brand in late 2020, moving it to a new look at Banana Republic called BR Standard. Gap supported the LGBTQIA lifestyle with its "Love Is Love" campaign in Banana Republic stores across the company during 2018 Pride (Figure 6.9). Other divisions such as Old Navy and Gap celebrated with their line of T-shirts, sweatshirts, and socks. In 2019 Gap celebrated over fifty years in business with such novelty items as a Ruth Bader Ginsburg "Dissent Collar" that sold out immediately. In 2019, the company acquired children's clothing company Janie and Jack, which it soon sold on in 2021.

Figure 6.9 Love is Love Campaign at the Banana Republic store in New York, 2018. (Photo courtesy of the author)

Figure 6.10 Gap promotes an extra 50 percent off an entire store of markdowns during COVID-19 to generate sales. (Photo courtesy of the author)

The company has not been without its peaks and valleys, and in 2020 with the onset of COVID-19, Gap closed more stores across the United States and promoted massive sales across the brands (Figure 6.10).

The company's move into the future is quite a unique approach. Gap has announced its plans to move into home décor, furniture, and textiles over the next three years to build a better lifestyle brand. The company recently signed a licensing deal with IMG and has plans for the Banana Republic to launch into new categories and GapKids to go into baby equipment and care products under their existing baby clothing brands.[15] The 1980s mall retailer also stated it would be moving away from traditional store formats and types. Gap will grow its Athleta division and has announced it will open twenty to thirty stores in Canada. The brand recently signed an agreement with world champion gymnast Simone Biles and hopes to encourage young women to rise and be seen!

On March 17, 2021, Gap announced it has billion-dollar ambitions for its Yeezy deal with Kanye West. This new celebrity Gap collaboration is a ten-year agreement, with Gap expecting this Yeezy line to make over $150 million in sales in its first full year in 2022.[16] The company hopes the brand will be worth a billion dollars, again demonstrating how Gap associations and collaborations with celebrities are what the company has become reliant on and are still a part of the vision it started in the late 1980s.

During the writing of this book, Gap reintroduced their Individuals of Style campaign, this time calling it GENERATION GOOD. Photographed by Mark Seliger, this campaign reimagines that good things can happen. Some of those highlighted are trans community leader D'Jamel Young, fourteen-year-old clean water activist and philanthropist Mari Copeny, 16-year-old anti-bullying activist and speaker Nandi Hildebrand, and more. Auroa James, a young celebrity designer, sums up the ideas of this campaign by stating, "I think the world is really ready for a rebirth and we're about to show how many beautiful colors we developed while we were cocooning. And we're really ready to take off and fly. And it's going to be really beautiful."[17]

Discussion Questions

1. Describe the similarities and differences between Gap, Uniqlo, H&M, and Zara. If you do not have the actual stores near you, utilize their social media websites. How are they the same, and how are they different? Describe how they present their products. Is it similar or different?

2. Shop Gap, Uniqlo, H&M, and Zara for a pair of jeans. How does each brand do jeans differently? Which brand fits you best as a customer? Why? Which of these fast fashion companies do you think presents denim in the most luxurious context? Describe how they do this.

3. What collaborations have Gap, Uniqlo, H&M, and Zara done in the past? Were they successful, or did they fail? Why?

4. Do you shop in fast fashion? Besides the price, why? If you know that fast fashion is a sustainability issue, what can you do that will allow you to be sustainable and still shop your favorite brands?

Expand Your Knowledge

The Gap Inc. states that it distinguishes between the various retail divisions. The company promotes a good, better, best strategy with Old Navy (Good), Gap (Better), and Banana Republic (Best) representing these types. Go on a shopping trip to Gap, Banana Republic, or Old Navy. Visit their men's or women's department and note the products' fashion styles, prices, quality, and the fabric content of each garment (what is it made of?). Are they similar or completely different in quality? Look at the quality both inside and outside the garment; for example, turn the garment inside out and see how it is sewn and the hems are finished. Is the quality better at the Banana Republic, Gap, or Old Navy? What product is each store emphasizing? Are they doing collaborations with designers? Write up your findings and share them with your colleagues.

Further Exploration

Watch:
Fast Company, *See The History of GAP in 4 Minutes* (2015), https://www.
   youtube.com/watch?v=zTuzOZtnVzo (accessed April 25, 2021).
Read:
Lard & Partners, *Individuals* (New York: Melcher Media, 2006), 7.

Chapter 7
Celebrity Collaborations and Philanthropy: MAC

Chapter Objectives

> Introduce the beauty industry with a short history of Estée Lauder
> Highlight MAC Cosmetics and its niche marketing strategies
> Discuss the significance of VIVA Glam and celebrity collaborations for product promotion and success
> Note the impact of philanthropy on the branding of cosmetic brands

Figure 7.0 MAC Creative Director Drew Elliott (left) with music icon Boy George (center) and transgender American model Amanda Lepore (right) celebrate Halloween while also representing the diversity of consumers MAC represents to differentiate itself from competitors. (Photo by JP Yim/Getty Images for MAC Cosmetics)

The cosmetics industry is quite significant in the world of fashion branding. It relies heavily on promotion that distinguishes one brand from another. One of the leading players, Estée Lauder, is the owner of over twenty-five leading beauty and retailing chains worldwide. The company has earned over $14 billion in sales and significant profit margins. The impact of the Estée Lauder brand is culturally significant in our global economy. This chapter relates Estée Lauder's story and one of its outstanding subsidiaries: Makeup Art Cosmetics, commonly known as MAC.

History of Estée Lauder

In the 1930s, Estée Lauter (who eventually changed her name to Lauder) founded the company when she began formulating and selling skincare products. With her Hungarian uncle John Schotz (who was the original expert), Lauder developed her face creams and cleaning oils. In 1944, with her husband Joseph Lauder, Estée was able to add lipsticks, eye shadows, and face powders. She was adamant about getting her products into department stores. She did so by offering samples and handouts for customers and enculturated the cosmetic ideology of *gift with purchase*. She traveled all over the country and eventually got her products into luxury department stores across the globe. She also held development seminars and taught everyone how to use the products.[1]

In 1953, Estée Lauder launched her first fragrance, Youth Dew, which included perfume and bath oil. Lauder's big break came during the late 1950s when American cosmetic companies decided to launch European skincare lines. The company developed Re-Nutriv cream, which sold for $115 per pound until 1960. The cream's advertising campaign "established the sophisticated Lauder look—an image that Estée Lauder herself cultivated."[2]

In 1968, Lauder launched Clinique, a hypoallergenic skincare line. She continued focusing on makeup and skincare, doing demonstrations with store personnel, professional models, and fashion designers on how to use her products (Figure 7.1). Eventually, Estée named her son Leonard president of the company, but Estée remained CEO as the prominent leader. In 1979, she developed Prescriptive skincare, a line of makeup for young professional women. In 1990, Lauder launched Origins; in 1991, she launched All Skins cosmetics, and in 1994 she bought a controlling stake in the hip Makeup Art Cosmetics. In 1998 Estée Lauder purchased the rest of MAC, and the rest is history.[3] In 2004, Estée Lauder died of a heart attack at the age of ninety-seven.

Figure 7.1 Estée Lauder demonstrates her products on a model during a Yves Saint Laurent Fashion Show, c.1966. (Public Domain Library of Congress Prints and Photographs Division, Washington, D.C. 20540 USA)

Estée Lauder Today

Today, the Estée Lauder company holds the beauty licenses of or owns the following companies: Arein Beauty, Aramis, Aveda, Bobbi Brown, Bumble and Bumble, Clinique, Coach, Darphin Paris, Donna Karan Cosmetics, Editions De Parfums Frédéric Malle, Ermenegildo Zegna, Estée Lauder, Flirt!, GLAMglow, Goodskin Labs, Jo Malone London, Kiton, La Mer, Lab Series, Le Labo, Marni, Michael Kors, Ojon, Origins, Osiao, Prescriptives, Rodin Olio Lusso, Smashbox, Tom Ford Beauty, Tommy Hilfiger, Tory Burch, and finally MAC. Fabrizio Freda, the CEO of Estée Lauder, has stated that over the last few years the company has seen steady revenue growth. Estée Lauder's plan for expansion is increasing its international markets and product portfolio; the company is trying to push brand awareness through its many divisions and is devoted to developing a better online presence to generate revenue. It is also increasing its product exposure on social media.

The company is expanding its makeup lines to differentiate itself from the competition and grow in the hair care arena through various retail outlets. Unlike many competitors, who turn to celebrities to promote brand awareness, Estée Lauder turns to fashion and retail. The company is focused on geographic growth in China, the Middle East, Eastern Europe, Brazil, and South Africa and customers who purchase through travel and retail channels such as duty-free stores in airports.[4]

Because of this growth strategy, Estée Lauder plans to incorporate its higher-priced goods in these international markets. The company will market its skincare lines because they are its most successful product category. In 2014 the company launched the Somaly Mam Beauty Salon in Cambodia and the Jo Malone London brand at the Mitsukoshi store in Beijing, China. The company currently sells its products in more than 150 countries. The United States is the largest consumer market (over 40 percent of sales) with Europe, the Middle East, and Africa accounting for only a little over 30 percent of sales.

A Short Brand/Story   **Branding Sneakers: Interview with Sean Williams**

Individuals across the world love sneakers. Sean Williams is a born and raised Brooklynite who fell in love with sneakers at the age of thirteen. By age sixteen, with a few years of work experience under his belt, he began buying sneakers with his own money (no longer asking mom for the latest and freshest kicks). Having purchased thousands of pairs of sneakers over the years, his love of sneakers has never ultimately died. It has simply transformed.

In 2007, Obsessive Sneaker Disorder (OSD, LLC) was founded by longtime friend Dee Wells and Sean was asked to become a part of the historical movement. OSD, LLC's mission is to educate the public on the importance of sneaker culture. Through his business partnership in OSD, Sean's love of sneakers has transformed into the company's mission, which has three words: "Appreciate, Educate, Elevate." These days, those three words are a part of everything Sean does regarding the world of sneakers. He has accepted the personal mission of making sure that the younger generations know the potential for them in the athletic footwear business as not only consumers but also future professionals in the industry. Sean has been featured in various noteworthy TV shows, publications, and websites such as NBC's *The Today Show*, *Maxim* magazine, *Slate.com*, and *Sneaker Freaker*, just to name a few. In 2012, Sean and his partner Dee made the list of "50 Most Influential People in Sneakers Right Now" published by *Complex* magazine. Sean also teaches OSD's "SOLEcial Studies," which is an education program that prepares people worldwide for potential jobs in the athletic footwear business. He has plans to begin teaching the program in partnership with sports teams and schools across the United States. The rest of his story is still being written, one sneaker at a time.

Why do consumers love sneakers?

To be honest, the love of sneakers wasn't always there. I can recall a time in the 1970s, perhaps earlier, when if you were not a student, into sports or hip-hop, people did not wear them as often as they do now. People were excessively judgmental of those who wore sneakers. There were a lot of places you couldn't enter if you had sneakers on your feet. Over time the love of sneakers has grown due to the emergence of hip-hop culture and its global influence. More people in America actively participate in sports both recreationally and professionally, and there has been an evolution in what is acceptable to wear in the workplace. Sneakers are now easier to wear in daily life and more important as part of the consumer experience.

Out of all the sneakers you own, do you have a favorite pair? Why is it the one?

My favorite pair of sneakers is the 1987 Nike Air Max 1 in the original red, gray, and white. It's the first sneaker I bought at the age of fifteen years, with my own money. It just happens to be one of the sneakers that changed the entire sneaker industry due to its revolutionary design.

Do athletic sneaker brands do a good job telling brand/stories to get consumers to buy? Which brand do you think does the best job?

On an industry-wide level overall, there are opportunities. They only scratch the surface of good stories or omit facts in some cases. I would not give any brand a best-in-class rating at this time. If you asked me this question ten years ago, I would say, Nike, Adidas, and Puma.

> **Where do you see the future of the sneaker industry going?**
> The sneaker industry has made a very conscious effort to embrace computer technology and data more. Unfortunately, it is coming at the expense of community-based retailers who helped many of these sneaker brands to be very profitable. A serious push for a direct-to-consumer experience is where most of the industry is trending.

Makeup Art Cosmetics: MAC

What keeps the Estée Lauder company thriving and growing is its unique brands representing various markets and cultural groups. MAC, one of its acquisitions, is a leader in this area. In the early 1970s, two artists from Ontario, Canada—Frank Toskan and Frank Angelo—and chemist Vic Casale developed and sold their line of makeup for fashion models. Their product line was revolutionary, designed to work with different skin colors and to reflect well on camera. It was significantly better than products that were then available for fashion photography and film. At the time, fashion professionals relied on heavy base cosmetics for the stage, screen, and visual effects. The makeup was thick and quite harmful to a model or actor's complexion.

Toskan and Angelo created something unique and unforgettable. Their line became known for its extensive range of colors and its individual pots of color, and innovation over the usual pre-packaged combinations.[5] Moreover, their makeup was not as heavy, nor did it have a pancaked feel. It was unique because it was easy to use. The makeup line grew in popularity, and the two decided they wanted to sell their products to the public. In 1985, they created the company Makeup Art Cosmetics, commonly called MAC.

The company has grown, and today you can buy MAC products in over seventy countries. It currently employs over twelve thousand makeup artists and is known for its mantra: "all ages, all races, all sexes." The company has fostered an environment in which everyone is free to be whoever they want to be and express who they are, and what better way to do it than through makeup? In addition to being a makeup choice for people of color because of its assortment of skin tones, MAC has become the brand synonymous with drag queens, gay men, lesbians, transgender people, rock stars, goths, punks, freaks, and those other historically marginalized markets. Each MAC employee serves these clients with respect and dignity, treating them as unique as the fashion models and movie stars the brand served in the 1970s—because, in the world of MAC, the customer is a star.

Philanthropic Branding with a Twist: VIVA GLAM

In the article "The Ringleader: M.A.C.: How a Weird Indie Startup Took Over the World of Makeup," writer Danielle Pergament begins with this:

> Imagine you're at a dinner party. And not just any dinner party. You're at a dinner party seated next to Catherine Deneuve, who, by the way, is ignoring you and talking to Raquel Welch. To your right is Nicki Minaj, telling off-color jokes with RuPaul. Just as the salad is served, the door bursts open, and Lady Gaga blows in, Elton John and Liza Minnelli right behind her. You look in the corner and see ... wait. Is that? Yes, there's Wonder Woman, discreetly picking a piece of spinach out of her teeth, while Barbie giggles next to her. And just when things can't get any weirder, you look across the table and lock eyes with Hello Kitty. She tilts her cartoon head and gives you a knowing look—one that says, Yep, welcome to M.A.C.[6]

"What kind of a company ignites its charity program by selling lipstick with RuPaul, a drag queen, as its spokesperson?" (Figure 7.2).[7] The answer is MAC. The Canadian brand has always been fearless and outspoken, and when it comes to the VIVA GLAM message, it's always been loud and clear.

In the mid-1990s, when most companies focused on supermodels, the founders of MAC concentrated on stopping the spread of HIV and AIDS. The VIVA GLAM campaign was a way to reach out to the world through the world of cosmetics. The idea was to start with a lipstick that resembled and had a symbiotic representation of a bullet to be the "shot fired round the world"[8] announcing that MAC was there to help those infected with HIV and AIDS. VIVA GLAM became the first philanthropic effort to give 100 percent of proceeds to help the cause. MAC wished to support awareness of HIV/AIDS because it was stigmatized as a "gay disease." The company conveyed, "We support everyone with HIV/AIDS, and it's not just a 'gay disease'—it impacts everyone." There is nothing held back at the helm of MAC.

By using RuPaul Charles as its spokesmodel for VIVA GLAM, MAC was making a statement. It was a return to gay rights and the notion that gays have a voice in the community, especially in fashion and cosmetics. It was the drag queens who started the gay rights movement at Stonewall on June 28, 1969. Famous drag queens such as Sylvia Rivera (1951–2002) and Marsha P. Johnson (1944–1992) led the fight for equality during

Figure 7.2 RuPaul attends MAC store opening in London, April 19, 1995. (Photo by Alexis DUCLOS/ Gamma-Rapho via Getty Images).

the Stonewall years.[9] Using a drag queen such as RuPaul (who had just released his single, *Supermodel (You Better Work)*), MAC was making a statement on not only gay rights but also on building awareness about HIV/AIDS. Many in the fashion world and makeup industry died from AIDS.

It is essential for today's readers, especially those in college and even perhaps in high school, to know that during the 1980s, many young individuals became infected with HIV/AIDS. Gay men and those with AIDS were often outcasts among their families and friends. People thought you could catch AIDS just from hugging someone with the disease. This disease was devastating and controversial because it happened in our own country, our backyards, and our friends and family members. Many lives were lost, and most individuals, especially in the gay communities, knew one or two people who had died of it. More importantly, there is no cure for HIV/AIDS, and infection still occurs.

> With 100 percent of the proceeds of every VIVA GLAM product going directly to men, women, and children affected by HIV/AIDS, it was an unparalleled move. The idea of VIVA GLAM was to celebrate life and the outspoken attitude of the company. It was a connective tissue that

encompassed the diversity of M.A.C. and its mantra … all ages, all races, all sexes. It was, and continues to be, the signature and the heart and soul of the company.[10]

Interestingly, Estée Lauder bought an interest in MAC the same year it launched the VIVA GLAM campaign. Perhaps she noted the importance of such a movement and knew that MAC was doing something revolutionary. Not only were its products phenomenal, but the company was blatantly supporting a consumer market that had been stigmatized and ostracized. Estée Lauder probably recognized that MAC addressed many consumers and was filling niche markets that historically were marginalized.

Celebrity Endorsement, Collaborations, and Genderless Boundaries

The idea of using celebrities to promote products is genius as it allows for both brands to collaborate and draw on both target markets. In a world of new products developed almost daily and the magnitude of social media growth, any competitive edge is essential for products to remain in the spotlight. Celebrities have become models personifying the brands they represent. As research suggests, celebrities can reinvent their careers through collaborations with products that can help them branch off into new business models.[11] The key is for the originating brand, in this case MAC, to choose the right celebrity.

VIVA GLAM spokespeople are provocative, alternative, and influential and reflect diverse communities. They are heroes we look up to for their personal triumphs, people who have invented themselves, and people who have created movements. Over the years, the list has included RuPaul, K.D. Lang, Mary J. Blige, Lil' Kim, Sir Elton John, Shirley Manson, Christina Aguilera, Missy Elliott, Linda Evangelista, Chloë Sevigny, Boy George, Pamela Anderson, Eve White, Lisa Marie Presley, Debbie Harry, Dita von Teese, Fergie, Lady Gaga, Cyndi Lauper, Ricky Martin, Nicki Minaj, Miley Cyrus, and Rihanna (Figure 7.3).[12]

Celebrating over twenty-five years in existence, VIVA GLAM continues and reflects fashion branding's future with its provocative way of addressing awareness. MAC was the first to take a stance on HIV/AIDS awareness, and consumers have voted through their purchases that this philanthropic action is still necessary for the battle against the disease. Since its inception, this fund has raised over $270 million by selling lipstick for $16.[13]

MAC's approach is phenomenal. The idea of giving 100 percent of all proceeds to charity is unique, with most companies giving a smaller percentage. As time has progressed, this approach has become less avant-garde because consumer markets accept the gay, lesbian, and transgender communities. But what is still unique about MAC is its marketing directed toward minorities of color, and it is capturing their consumer dollars at all times. While more cosmetic companies are marketing toward people of color, MAC did it first. It continues to bank on women of color such as Rihanna and Nicki Minaj to draw attention to its brand. At the time of writing this book, the singer Rosalía is the most recent VIVA GLAM face; we all know MAC will continue its unique approach of reaching all consumers with a new celebrity that out-of-the-box for the fashion industry in its next VIVA GLAM campaign.

Celebrating its ideology of inclusiveness, in 2019, MAC was at the forefront of initiating the doctrine of gender-neutral makeup for its consumer base. The customer experience's clear focus reflects the finding that 83 percent of millennial men thinking their appearance is significant, and over 52 percent of men agree that facial skincare brands

Figure 7.3 Rapper Nicki Minaj (left) and pop singer Ricky Martin tape an interview at *Good Morning America* at the ABC Times Square studios, New York City on February 15, 2012. (Photo by Ray Tamarra/Getty Images).

focus too much on women. To launch a global awareness campaign for all genders, MAC opened a pop-up shop in Liverpool, England. Located in the Liverpool ONE shopping center, the space's goal was to "celebrate all skin types" and hype self-expression among all makeup wearers. The company called its new product the Studio Fix Foundation Stick, and for five days it provided ten-day samples, personalized product demonstrations, and the company's new, innovative "We've Got You" kaleidoscopic mirror wall. This mirror allows for virtual try-on of makeup without the consumer actually applying the product to their face. The exterior of the shop was covered in images of individuals representing MAC's diverse clientele. It was a celebration for all ages, all races, and all genders. It was truly MAC![14]

Discussion Questions

1. Choose a division of Estée Lauder that is part of a fashion line. How does the line's particular fragrance reflect the brand it serves?
2. Do you wear fragrance or makeup? Why do you wear that particular fragrance or makeup? Does Estée Lauder own it?
3. How does VIVA GLAM give MAC a "good" name in the beauty industry? Why do you feel its philanthropic mission is good? Or do you think it is negative? Why? How would you improve this campaign?
4. Think of another retailer, brand, or fashion house that gives to a charity. Is it giving just as much as MAC or only a percentage? How much? What are your thoughts about that? Is it charity?

Expand Your Knowledge

Conduct a personal shopping experience by visiting your local department store. Go to the cosmetics or men's fragrance counter and identify all the brands that are part of the Estée Lauder group. Choose one. Next, pretend you are a customer and discuss one of the brands with the counter's selling professionals. See if they explain how to use the product and give you details of the product that make it unique. Did they convince you to buy the product? Or are you shopping for something you usually buy anyway? Why do you use that particular product? Ask the course instructor if you should get extra information. Do a two- to three-page report on the experience.

Further Exploration

Watch:
Bloomberg, *How Estée Lauder Is Building on a History of Diversity* (2018), https://www.youtube.com/watch?v=Sn92ZuUUv_U (accessed April 25, 2021).
MAC, *RuPaul for MAC 1995* (1995), https://www.youtube.com/watch?v=rPjDh7SrtkQ (accessed April 25, 2021).
MAC, *Viva Glam 25 MAC Cosmetics* (2019), https://www.youtube.com/watch?v=jeA14dRVZWQ (accessed April 25, 2021).

Chapter 8
Retro-Branding: Levi Strauss & Co.

Chapter Objectives

> Discuss the history of Levi Strauss & Co.
> Reveal when denim overalls become blue jeans
> Elaborate on the importance of Levi's 501 jeans as a critical item for the company
> Discuss the nostalgic and chronological brand strategy behind Levi's branding techniques

Figure 8.0 Levi Strauss, who became an American citizen in 1853. (Photo by ullstein bild/ ullstein bild via Getty Images)

Jeans are probably the most common garment found in everyone's wardrobe. They come in all fits and sizes and various types of fabric, including polyester, Lycra, modal, and even linen, so that they can be worn by all body types and in warmer climates. My most recent search for blue jeans was for my mother so that she could wear them as a poststroke disabled person: everything she wears has to have an elastic waist and be of a knit fabric so that she can pull them up and down without a problem. But thanks to Lands' End, I was able to find a pair of knit blue jeans, and she could not have been happier.

My mother has a special attachment to blue jeans, or, as most baby-boomers refer to them, Levi's. Being part of the youth culture movements of the 1950s–1970s, she understood the negative associations attached to jeans as a rebel garment, and, as she put it, "we fought hard to wear our jeans." But blue jeans are an American icon just as much as Coca-Cola and Pepsi, especially Levi's 501 jeans. Jeans are associated with many nostalgic ideologies, from gold mining to the hippie era's protests of the late 1960s and early 1970s. Jeans represent a uniform of nonconformity, as well as fitting into the mainstream. While Lee and Wrangler have dared to compete, no other jean has stood the test of time or been as well branded.

Levi's is now experiencing a resurgence and most recently has returned to its heritage with the Made in the USA Vintage line and the new 501CT, which has more of a tapered leg than the standard 501. Another use of heritage is the new DIY Customization process in which customers design and share their own Levi's designs via Twitter and Facebook.

Levi's jeans' assortment is endless, with just as many stories, fashion branding campaigns, and evolutions of style. Levi's has been a consumer market revolution extraordinaire. Forget the innovations and shocking ads of Abercrombie & Fitch or the risqué campaigns of Calvin Klein because Levi's is the innovator of jeans and the innovator of diversified brand/stories and marketing campaigns that have shocked millions. Levi's loves everyone and is one of the few brands that put their money where their mouth is. Levi's has always been a champion of popular culture.

History of Levi Strauss & Co.

There is a common mistaken notion that Levi Strauss invented denim jeans while working in a gold mine in California. Actually, Levi Strauss was born of German Jewish immigrants in 1829. At the age of eighteen, he and his two sisters moved to the United States to join his two brothers, who had started a wholesale dry goods business in New York

City called J. Strauss Brothers & Co. Later Levi Strauss moved to Louisville, Kentucky, to sell his brothers' dry goods.

Eventually, the family decided to open a branch of the dry goods business in San Francisco, and in 1853 Levi Strauss opened his wholesale dry goods business selling clothing and assorted household goods to small grocery stores across the West Coast. During the gold rush, miners needed strong enough pants to stand the strain of working in the mines. The style of pants they had been wearing would tear because of mining stress and tension.

So, in 1873 Levi Strauss and his partner Jacob Davis (a tailor from Reno, Nevada) applied for and received the official US Patent and Trademark (patent number 139,121) to own the right to make copper-riveted overalls in San Francisco. The first pairs of jeans were sewn and constructed from brown cotton duck and blue denim.[1]

During the last half of the nineteenth century, Levi Strauss & Co. ran advertising campaigns to sell its patented riveted clothing. With the slogan "The Best in Use for Farmers, Mechanics and Miners" (Figure 8.1), the garments were marked for this era's particular lifestyle. During this time, the iconic logo showing two horses trying to pull apart a pair of Levi's "waist overalls" became popular (Figure 8.2). The ideas behind

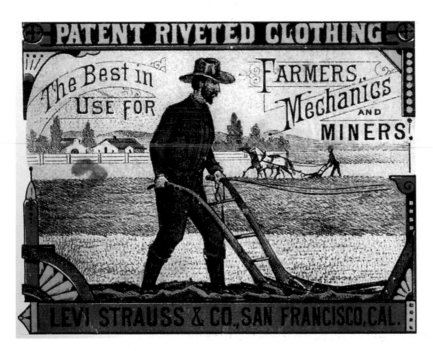

Figure 8.1 Advertisement for Levi Strauss & Co.'s copper-riveted overalls, c.1875. (Courtesy of the Advertising Archives)

Figure 8.2 Levi Strauss & Co.'s iconic two-horse logo that demonstrates the strength of the copper-riveted 501s. (Photo by Ullstein Bild Dtl. via Getty Images)

this early advertising led to an emphasis on authenticity, with the words "patented riveted clothing" demonstrating that Levi Strauss's "waist overalls" were indeed the first. In 1890, the iconic 501 got its name simply because this was the item number assigned to it as part of the Levi Strauss & Co. inventory. These same design details of riveted five pockets give the garment a feeling of authenticity, even though most Levi's jeans are no longer made in the United States.

In 1902, Levi Strauss died and left his company to his nephews, with his last request being that the company served Bay Area charities for children and the poor. In 1905, the company introduced khaki clothing into the product line for office apparel. In 1906, the Levi Strauss & Co. building was destroyed in the great San Francisco earthquake.[2]

In 1918, the company took its first stance in the women's rights movement by creating the first garment for women. They were called "freedom-alls" and were described as "a one-piece tunic over trousers for women to wear for both housework and outdoor leisure," with the word "freedom" implying that the garment allowed women to move freely. In 1928, the word *Levi's* was in danger of becoming a generic word for denim pants, so the company applied for a trademark to maintain name exclusivity.[3]

Denim Overalls Become Blue Jeans

In 1934, Levi's created the first pair of denim pants for women, and in 1936 the iconic red tab was introduced. In 1941, during the Second World War, Levi's jeans and jackets went global as US military soldiers wore their garments overseas while serving their country. That same year, Levi's took a stance on equal rights by integrating black workers into all its California manufacturing facilities.[4]

During the 1950s, denim pants became very popular and, like most fashions, were made famous through celebrity endorsements and styles.

Figure 8.3 Natalie Wood talks with James Dean on the set of the film *Rebel Without a Cause*, 1955. (Photo by Warner Brothers/Getty Images)

One person who popularized them was James Dean in the film *Rebel Without a Cause* (1955). His iconic look became an instant hit with young folks who idolized Dean (Figure 8.3), and his death before the release of the film popularized the look even more. Thanks to James Dean, the white T-shirt, red Baracuta jacket, engineer boots, and denim pants became the uniform of youth culture. Possibly because of the publicity given to denim pants in film, in 1959, Levi's began exporting its garments to Europe, where they became an international success.

Readers need to understand that it was because of denim having its big-screen debut that it became accepted by the masses. The ideology of rebellion is solidified in Marlon Brando in the 1953 movie, *The Wild One*. Brando personified the motorcycle-loving nonconformist, clad in jeans and a leather jacket, and brought this counterculture fashion into the mainstream. The Civil Rights movement began to unfold in the mid-1950s and ushered in over a decade of boycotts, sit-ins, and marches. Jeans were worn by some activists and became a symbol of protest for the movement. In April 1962, the town of Huntsville, Alabama, protested segregation in department stores by replacing Easter Sunday with "Blue Jean Sunday." Clothing stores were estimated to have lost a million dollars in the boycott.

Street Style Influence: Interview with Brent Luvaas

 Many fashion enthusiasts are always discussing how they are going to start a fashion blog or how they want to use social media to let everyone know that their sense of fashion or their words of wisdom on style need to be heard by the entire world … so they contemplate how to get on social media to let everyone know. Brent Luvaas is associate professor of anthropology at Drexel University. He is the author of *Street Style: An Ethnography of Fashion Blogging* (Bloomsbury, 2016) and *DIY Style: Fashion, Music, and Global Digital Cultures* (Bloomsbury, 2013). More importantly, he is known for his street style photography and is the blogger behind Urban Fieldnotes (www.urbanfieldnotes.com). He started his blog as a way to ethnographically study the phenomenon of street style blogging and is here to share his ideas on street style, fashion branding, and blogging.

Tell us why street style has become such a hot topic and so crucial in the twenty-first century

Street style has been around for as long as people have been wearing clothing on the streets, and photographers have been capturing it since the invention of the camera. But street style has become a hot topic in recent years for one simple reason: the blog. Back in 2005, Liisa Jokinen and Sampo Karjalainen started what is most likely the first independent street style blog, *Hel Looks*, to document the sartorial idiosyncrasies of "regular" people on the streets of Helsinki, Finland. It was followed by Scott Schuman's *The Sartorialist* in New York several months later and Tommy Ton's *Jak & Jil* soon after that. By 2006, street style blogs were popping up in big cities throughout the world, representing style in places well off the fashion map and attracting hundreds of thousands of readers. The fashion industry began to take notice, and soon bloggers like Schuman and Ton had signed contracts with Condé Nast and other fashion publishers to take "street style" pictures outside runway shows at the major fashion events in New York, Paris, Milan, and London. Street style quickly evolved into the fashion-marketing machine that it is today. Go to a show by any well-known designer at any fashion week worldwide and a crowd of street style photographers hovers near the entrance, stopping rising street style stars in brand-loaned couture. Street style has gone from an amateur practice of documenting the everyday looks of regular people around the globe to a professional documentation of fashion industry insiders, marketing both the clothes they are wearing and their own personal brand.

Does branding reflect notions of street style, or are they two completely different areas of fashion?

Street style today is permeated through and through with the logic of branding. PR companies loan clothes to street style stars for them to wear to shows. Editors negotiate with clothing labels months before fashion week to find their own outfits for the events. Street style photographers use their blogs to build their own professional brands. And designers often look to the photos they take to find inspiration for their latest collections. Street style has become a significant part of the fashion industry branding process.

How do you believe your work has influenced the world of branding and/or street style?

My work hasn't influenced the world of branding and/or street style at all, unless you count the many conversations I've had with street style bloggers, giving them a chance to reflect on what it is that they do. From the beginning, I have approached my work on street style photography not as some mighty academic observing from above and judging from on high, but as a photographer myself, a peer, engaging in the very same work they do, and building my understanding of street style and its practice in continual dialogue with other street style photographers.

How does and will technology continue to play a key role in the world of street style and brands?

   Digital cameras and free online publishing platforms, i.e., blogs, made street style into the phenomenon it is today. But blogs are rapidly losing their relevance. Today, social media platforms, including Twitter, Snapchat, TikTok, and Tumblr, and especially Instagram, have become go-to resources for street style photographers and fans alike. Why go to a blog, after all, if you can have its content come to you?

What are your words of advice for those who wish to work as a fashion blogger or street style photographer?

Don't do it. The market is already super-saturated. You really should have jumped on that bandwagon ten years ago. But if you must, then find some way to make your work stand out. Find your own spin. Do your own thing. And make sure your images feel like an authentic representation of who you really are.

Making Statements: 501 Jeans and Brand/Story

As the social revolution continued to dominate the 1960s, denim-clad rebels adopted jeans to embody the changing times. Jeans were an essential wardrobe piece of the movement that protested the Vietnam War, questioned their parent's values and the government, redefined gender roles, and fought for social progress. But the word *jeans* only became popular in the 1960s. Teenagers began calling their denim pants jeans, and eventually, Levi's replaced the word *overalls* with *jeans* on all their advertising and labels.[5]

During this time, with the enactment of the Civil Rights Act of 1960 that prohibited voting obstruction and introduced penalties to anyone not allowing someone to vote, Levi's introduced its first integrated manufacturing facility in the American South. The company continued to participate in progressive social movements by featuring such rock bands as Jefferson Airplane and Paul Revere & The Raiders in its radio ads. Levi's became the advertising leader and was known for its innovative ads celebrating gender equality, market diversity, and inclusiveness.

In the 1970s, to support the women's rights movement, Levi's reinvented an iconic film scene to release 501 blue jeans for women. Instead of a male ranch hand, Levi's featured a female in the same pose as James Dean in the film *Giant* (1956) (Figure 8.4). Dean's character in this film was known for being a rugged, tough, self made man, independent, mouthy, and somewhat arrogant, but a dedicated worker. By assigning this look to a female character, the company was suggesting the same qualities, stating that women are just a tough as men.

Abercrombie & Fitch and Calvin Klein are considered the big brands that sexualized men in the latter half of the twentieth century, but Levi's was right there, and its ads were scandalous. John Hegarty's 1985 Laundrette campaign for Levi's 501 Shrink-To-Fit Jeans featured the famous male model, Nick Kamen.[6] Kamen, a British male model and then unknown, was seen in what appears to be a beefcake ad in a 1950s laundrette television commercial. While Marvin Gaye's "I Heard It Through the Grapevine" plays, Kamen strips off his blue jeans in public and puts them in a washing machine. Women gawk, and men look on while Kamen ignores everyone. After he casually puts his clothes into the machine, he reaches for a magazine and sits down among all those who have been staring at him (Figure 8.5).

Figure 8.4 Levi's release of 501 blue jeans for women in 1970 reflecting the iconic 1956 film *Giant*. (Courtesy of Retro AdArchives via Alamy)

Figure 8.5 Nick Kamen in the famous 1985 Laundrette television advertisement for Levi's 501. (Courtesy of Advertising Archives)

Levi's ran the ad on Boxing Day (the day after Christmas) to obtain exchanges and more sales. The winning formula is key to a commercial on television using the theory of brand/story. The three significant elements of this ad: music, model, and mood, set the narrative stage. The music was Marvin Gaye's *I Heard it Through the Grapevine,* a song that was

No. 1 on the Billboard's 100 for R&B singles in 1968. The tune is iconic and almost immediately recognizable, making it a wonderful tie-in to the context of an ad. The model, Nick Kamen, was the eye candy for the viewer, women loved him and men wanted to be him. His charismatic looks made the sales of 501's skyrocket almost 800 percent according to a retail analyst. Finally, the mood of the scene, small-town America in the late 1950s or early 1960s with an army soldier was genius, allowing the Levi's brand a nostalgic post-modernistic feel, with the music inaccurate as well as the model. But the combined elements left the viewer feeling as if they were experiencing true American culture, when in reality it was a fantasy. That makes for an excellent hypermodern brand/story. This ad was seen as so risqué for the time that some stations refused to play it. But it competed with the designer jeans industries and helped Levi's sell 501 blue jeans. The ad eventually received the award as number 6 in the top 100 Greatest TV Ads of 2000. Nick Kamen passed away of bone marrow disease on May 4, 2021, just fifty-nine years old, but his legacy in this Levi's advertisement will live on.

In addition to using product endorsement for 501 blue jeans, during the 1980s, Levi's became the first company to sponsor an AIDS Walk and initiate a comprehensive HIV/AIDS program to educate its employees. The company launched the Dockers brand in 1986. It moved into the 1990s as one of the first multinational companies to establish and enforce labor rights and health and safety standards with all the vendors who manufacture its clothing. In 1993, the company continued its innovative advertising through campaigns such as "Women Breaking the Mold" with *Advertising Age*, which named it one of the best ads in the past fifty years. In 1994, *Fortune* magazine gave Levi's the award for the most admired apparel company.[7]

Ten years after the laundrette advertisement for 501 jeans, Levi's took another turn toward diversity. While some ads featured beefcakes, aliens, and women robbing banks, an iconic commercial that stood out from the rest was the Taxi Cab ad. A cab is coming down the avenue in what appears to be New York City and pulls up to let in a beautiful Filipino woman in for a ride (Figure 8.6).

The cabbie is stereotyped as an unshaven, greasy, old Caucasian male wearing a dirty white underwear tank top and holding a toothpick in his teeth. The cabbie keeps looking into the back as the attractive woman applies makeup and looks in her compact mirror. The cab driver obviously finds her very sexy. As the cab speeds past other cars, their passengers also stare at the beautiful woman. Suddenly the woman notices stubble on her chin and takes out a men's electric shaver. She begins to start shaving her face. It becomes clear, the woman is actually a man! The cab

Figure 8.6 Taxi Cab ad for Levi's 501 blue jeans starring Filipino fashion icon Zaldy Goco. (Courtesy of Advertising Archives)

comes to a screeching halt, the passenger gets out of the taxi and struts off, while the caption for the ad reads, "Cut for Men Since 1850, Levis 501. The Original Jean."[8]

The star of this ad is the late 1980s club kid and now famous RuPaul Drag Race three-time Emmy award-winning designer, Zaldy Goco. Zaldy dabbled in drag when he moved to New York to attend the Fashion Institute of Technology. Designers Thierry Mugler, Jean-Paul Gaultier, and Vivienne Westwood loved having Zaldy as one of their runway models for women's wear. His modeling controversy rose into the spotlight when he did the 1995 Levi's Taxi Cab ad. This tongue-in-cheek ad demonstrates Levi Strauss & Co.'s commitment to inclusiveness by recognizing transgender communities. While we do not know if the individual is transgender or a drag queen, the commercial suggests both. Moreover, the use of such a brand/story demonstrates that Levi's feels this product applies to all communities, no matter who you are. By putting advertising dollars into such a campaign, the company declares that it supports anyone who wears its products. And by using Zaldy Goco, Levi's made a huge fashion statement and the brand in and of itself became associated with fashion insiders who knew Zaldy and his networks.

Over the next two decades, Levi Strauss & Co. continued to support such initiatives as reducing greenhouse gases, conserving water resources, and caring for the planet. The company has joined better cotton initiatives and supports cotton grown using sustainable practices. It continues to improve on all initiatives related to the environment.[9]

Sales, Strategy, and a Return to Heritage

Levi's continues to be a multichannel marketer with more than fifty thousand retail locations in over 110 countries. Leading department and chain stores such as JCP (JCPenney), Kohl's, Walmart, Target, Macy's, Nordstrom, and Barneys carry the brand. Levi's even creates private lines for retailers such as Target, where it sells its Denizen line in over 1,700 locations. Levi's maintains a competitive advantage over the other denim-carrying companies with sales of $4.5 billion.[10]

The company maintains over 208 stores in the United States, 201 in Europe, and 120 in Asia and the Pacific regions. It has opened its Levi's Lot No. 1 made-to-order jeans in London, where it customizes a handmade pair of jeans for each customer. This program has also expanded to the United States. The company continues to stress its ideology of being an originator.

With the revival of heritage brands for both men and women and the idea of sustainability Levi's has returned to its roots, invoking a feeling of retro-branding and authenticity. It manufactures historically significant garments such as the Triple Pleat Blouse Denim Jacket, designed and crafted initially in 1873. And now it sells secondhand clothing via its website to consumers at top dollar. A pair of secondhand corduroy pants from Levi's sells for between $78 and $118. In other words, it's not necessarily a thrift store, but instead a premium-priced authentic Levi's online warehouse where you can feel as if you are purchasing a piece of history. The company also has a customized online shop, a tailor shop, as well as Levi's Made & Crafted, Vintage Clothing, Premium and their cross collaborations. The company features the complete line of its 501 jeans, and you can order them from 1933, 1944, 1947, 1954, 1955, 1966, and 1978; each retails for about $260, and while the brand still specializes in men's, youth, and boy's apparel, the lines all feature women's clothing. The company now represents Levi's, Dockers, Denizen, and Signature with each of these divisions having their own unique target markets. But one thing is clear, the Levi's 501 jean is still the number one and the most noted of the company's contributions to brand/story success.

Discussion Questions

1. Why do you think everyone associates blue jeans with American culture?
2. Do you own a pair of Levi's jeans? If so, what fit do you own and why? If not, what brand do you prefer and why?
3. Why do you think Levi's is such a dominant brand in the consumer market? Do you feel that another brand is just as iconic? Which brand is it?

Expand Your Knowledge

Go to any search engine and look up a Levi's commercial from the past, then watch that commercial. What do you think about it? What consumer group is Levi's trying to reach and why? Do you feel the ad represents the brand? If yes, why? If no, why not? Write a two- to three-page paper about this ad and share it with the class.

Further Exploration

Watch:
Levi Strauss & Co., *The 501® Jean: Stories of an Original/Full Documentary* (2016), https://www.youtube.com/watch?v=6R9cAoCyatA (accessed April 25, 2021).
Read:
Levi Strauss & Co., *This Is a Pair of Levi's Jeans* (San Francisco, CA: Levi Strauss & Co. Publishing, 1995).

Chapter 9
Branding Affordable Eyecare: Warby Parker

Chapter Objectives

> Discuss the characteristics of the eyewear market in size and scope
> Reveal the difference between Warby Parker and its competitors
> Understand how and why Warby Parker's social media presence inspires trust among its consumers
> Explain the "buy one get one" concept and the impact on the Warby Parker brand

Figure 9.0 (*left to right*) Co-founder of Warby Parker Dave Gilboa, actor Ashton Kutcher, and co-founder of Warby Parker Neil Blumenthal attend Warby Parker LA Launch at Confederacy, Los Angeles on November 1, 2011. (Photo by Charley Gallay/WireImage)

Sunglasses and eyeglasses not only serve a functional aspect of our appearance; they also serve as fashion accessories and reflections of our identity and appearance management. This industry is estimated to be worth over $140 billion and will reach over $197 billion by 2027. Currently, eyeglass frames and sunglasses alone represent over $30 billion of the eyewear market, with sunglasses representing about $18 billion of the total market.[1]

The Eyeglasses Market

Eyeglasses are created and manufactured by a small number of large companies. To understand this market, it is essential to know who the key players are and their products. Merchandisers must also understand the eyewear markets because most fashion designers and luxury brands carry sunglasses as a critical entry point for consumers to buy into the brand. Cologne, handbags, and eyewear are usually three of the most purchased items. This chapter summarizes some of the key brands in the eyeglasses markets and then focuses on Warby Parker, the new twenty-first-century approach to selling mass fashion eyeglasses.

Luxottica

The Luxottica Group carries and represents the perceived luxury end in the eyewear market, selling both sunglasses and prescription eyeglasses. This company has earned over $8.7 billion. Sales continue to increase, with comparative sales growing since the start of the COVID-19 pandemic.[2] Estimations show that over 500 million consumers wear Luxottica brands, with almost 60 percent of all sales occurring in North America.[3]

This brand dominates their market. The company owns retail locations across the United States, including such famous names as Pearle Vision, Lens Crafters, Sunglass Hut, Oliver Peoples, Target Optical, and Sears Optical. Luxottica owns an insurance program known as EyeMed vision insurance. But the company is better known for selling such famous designer frames as Alain Mikli, Arnette, Eye Safety Systems, K&L (Killer Loop), Luxottica, Mosley Tribes, Oakley, and Vogue. The company also enters into license agreements with designer names such as Giorgio Armani, Bvlgari, Chanel, Ralph Lauren, Prada, Brooks Brothers, Burberry, Chaps, Coach, and Dolce & Gabbana.[4]

Silhouette International and Viva International

Established in 1964, Silhouette International, an Austria-based business, is known for its unique lightweight and rimless designs. Its goal is to market eyewear as a fashion accessory. This company is active with social media and utilizes Twitter, Facebook, and other promotional portals. The company is known for the Silhouette kiosk, which enables customers to try on their eyewear virtually. Silhouette only sells Silhouette brand glasses.

Viva International is an American-based company that has been in business since 1978. It is a subsidiary of the insurance company Highmark, and its products are distributed through the optometrist retailer Visionworks. The company represents such brands as Magic Clip, Savvy, and Viva and has license agreements with Bongo, Candie's Catherine Deneuve, GANT, GANT by Michael Bastian, GANT Rugger, and Guess? The company is known for inventing the famous Magic Clip Eyewear, which are sunglass lenses that clip onto the front of your eyeglasses.[5]

Marchon and Safilo

Marchon Brands, founded in 1983, is an American company that manufactures and distributes eyewear. It is owned by Vision Service Plan (VSP), with the retailing divisions distributing eyeglasses to many department stores, eyewear retailers, and boutiques, as well as duty-free shops. This company sells an estimated 16 million frames annually. It sells such brands as Airlock, Tres Jolie, X Games, Marchon NYC, and Flexon. It also licenses brands such as Calvin Klein, Calvin Klein Jeans, ck Calvin Klein, Chloe, Michael Kors, Valentino, Nine West, Dragon, and Emilio Pucci.[6]

Safilo, founded in 1934, is the second-largest manufacturer of eyewear and the international leader in luxury frames. The company, based in Italy, is vertically integrated, designing, manufacturing, and distributing all its products. Company sales have reached over $1.6 billion, with almost 75 percent of those in prescription frames. The company sells approximately 45 percent of its products in the United States. The brands include Carrera, Oxydo, Polaroid, Safilo, and Smith Optics. The company also licenses such names as Alexandar McQueen, Banana Republic, Bottega Veneta, Boss, Boss Orange, Hugo Boss, Christian Dior, and Fossil.[7]

Charmant, Marcolin, and De Rigo

Charmant Group, founded in Japan in 1956, manufactures and distributes eyewear globally. This company is the leader in the pure titanium frames market. House brands include Ad Lib, Aristar, Charmant Line Art, Charmant Titanium Perfection, and Valmax. The company has licensing agreements with Elle, Esprit, Puma, and Trussardi.Marcolin, founded in 1961, is an Italian company based in Milan that makes luxury eyewear. Marcolin is known for its unique design base established in fashion trends and style. Production has totaled over 5 million eyeglasses with sales over $220 million per year and 14 percent comparative sales. The company is known for releasing over seven hundred new models in a single year. It produces such brands as Marcolin and Web Eyewear, with license eyewear including Tom Ford, Timberland, 55DSL (Diesel), Diesel, Balenciaga, Dsquared2, Hogan, John Galliano, Roberto Cavalli, and CoverGirl. Another Italian eyewear company is De Rigo, founded in 1978. Distributing its products in over eighty countries, mainly in Europe, Asia, and South America, it is the third-largest eyewear company with brands such as Police, Lozza, and Sting. Its license brands include Blumarine, Carolina Herrera, Carolina Herrera New York, Chopard, Ermenegildo Zegna, Escada, Givenchy, and Fila.[8]

A Short Brand/Story

A Branding King of Retail Operations: Interview with Michael J. Edwards

Michael J. Edwards is a massive influence in the world of retail operations. Not always seen as the "sexy" side of the business, operations is the area that makes retailers profitable and successful. It is also where many retailing presidents start as they work their way to the top. Michael J. Edwards is currently an Independent Director, Chairperson of the Digital Technology Committee, and Investment Committee Member at Central Garden & Pet. Edwards served as President and CEO of Hanna Andersson, a leading digital-first apparel and lifestyle brand from 2019 to 2020. Before Hanna Andersson, he was Chief Executive Officer of online bag retailer eBags.com. From 2012 to 2015, Mr. Edwards was the Global Chief Merchandising Officer of Staples. From 2009 to 2011, Edwards was the Executive Vice President and Chief Merchandising Officer of Borders Group, Inc. He currently serves as a member of the Drexel University board. He previously served as a director of Flexsteel Industries, Inc. Mr. Edwards has been a senior executive at several major retailers and has significant experience with e-commerce's transformational impact on consumers, retailers, and suppliers.

What has been the biggest challenge you ever faced as a retail leader?

It was hands down running the Borders Group during the massive digital disruption that impacted music, movies, and books. The transformation to digital media and online shopping made the traditional book superstores not as relevant; this killed the business model of conventional profitability. As a result, sales plummeted, capital dried up, and the organization could not culturally adjust to the consumer's new age expectations. I took the company through Chapter 11 then, tragically, Chapter 7 liquidation. I had to lay off almost 18,000 associates, which was heartbreaking.

Where do you see retail/brands going in the next five years?

It depends on how big online shopping will be of the total retail spend in the future. In 2020 21 percent of total sales were done online. COVID-19 jump-started the massive shift. However, the question is, does it mature over the next five years, and at what level? The growth online has a direct impact on the number and type of stores needed or are relevant in the future. All brands will have to have a digital-first culture that serves today's consumers' modern needs any way they shop using current and future technology. Brands that master consumer data and create unique products and services will win in the marketplace. Leaders will have to think global and local in addressing market demands and opportunities.

What do you think the best characteristics of a retail leader are and will be needed?

To me, it always starts with an entrepreneurial attitude and value system. The best merchants balance analytics with creative passion and energy. Also, moving fast, handling volatility, and staying optimistic are keys to a long successful career. It's a people and team-based environment, so learning to be self-directed and collaborative is a highly critical skill set. You have to focus on delivering sales and margin performance every day and live under constant pressure in the ever-changing world of consumer tastes and trends. Finally, you have to understand and leverage technology/data in every part of the retail experience. Today's merchants have to be digital-savvy to create fantastic shopping experiences.

What advice would you give someone today about retailing career opportunities?

Today is a new day in retailing—it is a wholly disrupted business model. That is when the most incredible opportunities come to bear for those willing to take bold risks. If you love innovating, marketing, consumer experiences, developing products and services, this is the time to make retail your career. After thirty-eight years in the business, I have never seen this level of global transformation. This is the time for the next generation of leaders to make their mark on the industry and society.

Doing Things Differently: Warby Parker

Warby Parker is an independent eyewear company that is vertically integrated: it designs, manufactures, facilitates distribution, and sells its frames, with all production points in-house. The company began retailing eyeglass frames online in 2010. It all started when the company's founders, Neil Blumenthal, Andrew Hunt, David Gilboa, and Jeffrey Raider, went looking for reasonably priced yet fashionable eyeglasses and found none. The program began as a university project for the Wharton School of Business at the University of Pennsylvania. The four young men received $2,500 as seed money to start their project. The company got its name from two characters, Warby Pepper and Zagg Parker, who appeared in a journal by the writer Jack Kerouac.[9]

The company began strictly online with a philanthropic program of "Buy a Pair, Give a Pair." The company produces another pair of eyeglasses for each pair of eyeglasses it sells. The donated glasses go to a nonprofit organization called VisionSpring.[10] Warby Parker founder Neil

Blumenthal got his start at VisionSpring and firmly believes in corporate social responsibility (CSR).

With only an online presence in 2010, the company devised a unique program similar to the early Netflix program, which sent DVDs through the mail. It would send a box of four or five styles of eyeglasses through the mail so that consumers could try them on, a radical approach for older consumers or those with disabilities who could not leave their homes to shop. The company then extended this unique service to all US consumers, thereby reaching those who like shopping from home as well as those who may be disabled or elderly.

The company went from an online presence to social media and eventually to brick-and-mortar locations in Atlanta, New York City, Los Angeles, San Francisco, and Boston. The company has showroom installations in Philadelphia, Oklahoma City, Chicago, Miami Beach, Charleston, Nashville, Dallas, and Richmond, Virginia. A Warby Parker store combines the distinguished style of a traditional optometrist with a modern retailer's sophisticated style. The stores have their unique flavors, representing libraries and others representing cool lounges for social gatherings (Figure 9.1). Regardless, the eyeglasses are the center of attention in all locations.

Warby Parker aims to deliver retro-looking, higher-quality, better-looking prescription eyewear starting at $95, a fraction of the average price. This could appeal to those who would replace their glasses more

Figure 9.1 A general view of the atmosphere at Warby Parker's store in The Standard, Hollywood, in Los Angeles. (Photo by Michael Buckner/Getty Images for Warby Parker)

often if they were not so expensive.[11] One might say that Warby Parker is a twenty-first-century version of Gap, but for eyeglasses. Not surprisingly, one of its most prominent investors is Millard Drexler, current president of J.Crew, who changed the face of Gap during the 1980s. Drexler probably realized that the business model of Warby Parker was similar to Gap's and that it would succeed by catering to a mass market that sought fashionable eyeglasses but at a lower market price.[12]

Like Gap, Warby Parker is changing the eyewear market through private-label merchandise. Like the 1980s retailer, Warby Parker is knocking off high-priced designer frames for less, but it never wavers on quality, giving consumers what they desire. The company seems to cluster itself among retailers who promote mass fashion and fall under the ideology of masstige fashion and style, such as H&M, Uniqlo, Target, and Zara. What is important to note is that this brand has become almost a cheap chic brand itself. Buying from Warby Parker is remarkable because of its philanthropic ideology and quality. It has become celebrated by hipsters and those who cherish fashion and style.

Warby Parker Moving Forward with Vision

In 2021, Warby Parker's valuation could have been $3 billion.[13] The company has done this by operating on some basic ideology:

1 Treat customers the way we'd like to be treated.
2 Create an environment where employees can think big, have fun, and do good.
3 Get out there.
4 Green is good.[14]

The company believes in being transparent with its customers, giving them as much information as possible on its history of "Buy a Pair, Give a Pair," design, and culture. It builds relationships with customers utilizing Twitter, Facebook, and its blog. It is no wonder that the company is growing and continues to be successful. While catering to elderly customers with home delivery, the company also reaches all younger consumers with its social network ability. Younger consumers are concerned about whom they are buying from, and Warby Parker creates its perceived identity through social networks. The company puts on its best face on social media.

Warby Parker also advertises and has done so on television with a commercial that featured walking eyeballs.[15] The commercial educates consumers on how Warby Parker can keep its eyeglasses at a much lower price than its competitors by manufacturing and selling directly, cutting out the middleman. These commercials continue to represent the genre of film director Wes Anderson. They reflect the company founders' geek chic style, featuring retro glasses, intellectual individuals, and a dedication to culture through books and learning. Warby Parker makes "the geek" cool again and does so in style, capitalizing on the increasing popularity of this look with hipsters.

Falling from B Corp Status

Many companies in today's market thrive on being B Corp status, or in layman's terms, *public benefit corporations*. Such vital players include Unilever's Ben & Jerry's, Patagonia, and Gap's Athleta. These companies look at the big picture and focus on the good of humanitarian traits instead of just looking at profits as the bottom line. These firms must do good and strive to maintain an equilibrium with ethical sourcing, manufacturing, and consumption. These companies do not just put profits first.

As Warby Parker grew, the company no longer maintained its B Corp status, striving to raise $75 million in venture capital funds. The concerns over the future of Warby Parker focus on the notion of it wanting to obtain a publicly owned company status. Can the company and its management maintain a balance of profits with the most ideological sustainable version? Most financial theorists would argue this is not possible. In the simple explorations of Warby Parker, the answer is sadly "no." However, Warby Parker continues to do good work and with a purpose, regardless of whether they meet the technical standards for B Corp certification. Warby Parker has achieved high growth and now profitability while expanding its "buy one get one" program focused on providing eye care for students in low-income schools in New York City and Baltimore (the "Pupils Project").[16]

COVID-19: Being There for Consumers

In keeping its mission to do good work, the company held its stores open during the COVID-19 global pandemic. As national, state, and local governments deemed optometrists "essential workers," Warby Parker kept their stores open while many other optometrists closed to the public (Figure 9.2). They did this by following stringent health codes requiring customers to make advance appointments and wait outside

Figure 9.2 Warby Parker Store, King of Prussia Mall, Pennsylvania, United States. Note the employees and guests wear masks during the COVID-19 pandemic of 2020. (Courtesy of the author)

until called into the store. During the visit, each time a customer tries on glasses, they are placed in a sanitation tray for sterilizing. After a simple visit to the store, the eyeglasses arrive in the mail, a perfect fit thanks to the help received in store.

But what will the future be for Warby Parker? It is hard to know where a brand that started in 2010 will be in the next fifteen or twenty years, but at the moment, it is pretty successful. Moving forward, the brand will have to continue to reinvent itself and become aware of those who try to "knock it off." With an estimated worth of close to 3 billion dollars, there is an opportunity for another Warby Parker-inspired company to flourish as well.

Discussion Questions

1. Who are the key players in the eyewear market? Do you own glasses from any of these companies? If so, explain why and where you purchased them. If not, explain where you bought your last pair of glasses and from whom. Who is the manufacturer of those glasses?
2. What has Warby Parker done that is so unique? How does Warby Parker produce glasses at a much lower price?
3. Warby Parker believes that "green is good" and yet encourages the repurchasing of its eyewear by offering them at a lower price. How does a company that promotes low prices and the frequent purchase of a more affordable product support a sustainable environment?

Expand Your Knowledge

Go on a shopping spree for sunglasses at your local mall, department store, or campus shop. How many different brands and styles can you find (identify at least ten to fifteen), and how many different styles are there (identify at least ten)? What are the price ranges for sunglasses in your local area? Why are they priced differently? Is there a difference in quality? Are the lenses unique? Write an essay that reflects your finding.

Further Exploration

Watch:
Today Show, *Warby Parker Founders Earned Millions by Making Glasses More Affordable* (2016), https://www.youtube.com/watch?v=AWRF2wvUDxQ (accessed April 25, 2021).
Read:
Lawrence Ingrassia, *Billion Dollar Brand Club (How Dollar Shave Club, Warby Parker, and Other Disruptors Are Remaking What We Buy)* (New York: Henry Holt and Co., 2020).

Chapter 10
Rebranding American Manufacturing: Shinola

Chapter Objectives

- Review the importance of Shinola as signifying an American brand
- Discuss the importance of quality over quantity products
- Discuss the controversy over Shinola and being *Made in the USA*
- Reveal how one company can collaborate with other domestic companies to establish a brand image

Figure 10.0 Shinola's advertisement demonstrating how it uses everyday people in its brand campaigns. (Courtesy of Shinola)

In today's world of disposable fashion, creating high-quality products is not easy, but Shinola has done it. This company has revolutionized the world of watchmaking (as well as other products) and, at the same time, is educating employees through retraining programs. Those who had lost their jobs during Detroit's declining auto industry had an option to manufacture watches.

But now, after over five years in the business, has Shinola truly made a difference, or was it all just lip service? This chapter discusses a few of Shinola's impacts on Detroit, Michigan's economy and investigates their philosophy of production and giving back to the community. We will also look at some controversy over the watch manufacturer, with naysayers feeling the brand is doing nothing but paying lip service to helping others. But one can say, after successfully opening stores globally, a hotel, and diversifying the brand into new categories, Shinola must be doing something right.

I first discovered Shinola when shopping on Michigan Avenue in Chicago. While perusing a watch counter, an anxious selling professional appeared, saying, "Do you know about Shinola watches?" I had never heard of the company, but by the time he had explained Shinola's brand/story, I desired not just one but two watches. This sales professional's love of the brand and his story of how Shinola was hiring American workers and supporting the US labor market made me want to own the watches.

I started my collection of Shinola watches with its basic 47-mm Runwell model with a green face and maple leather strap. I also purchased the 46-mm Brakeman watch with a white face and black alligator strap. Over time, my collection has grown to include a limited-edition Henry Ford Pocket Watch (I own 819 out of 1,000 issued), two of the company's limited-edition Black Friday watches (recollecting the day after Thanksgiving in the United States), a wall clock, a desk clock, as well as over sixteen more wristwatches in different colors. One might say that I am a Shinola junky.

Each time I purchase a Shinola, I cannot wait to get home, open the Shinola wooden box that each watch comes in, and examine all the wonderful marketing pieces that go with it. Not only is the product high quality, but the packaging is phenomenal. This company has left no stone unturned. Shinola understands how to make each customer feel important, both in and out of the store. No detail is lost; Shinola gives customers leather care balm for cleaning the strap. It is a branding genius, but in this case, not only because of the brand package—this is an excellent moderate product that each wearer would be proud to own.

History of Shinola

The *Economist* article titled "Mo' time for Motown" lightheartedly retells the history of Shinola. Tom Kartsotis, the founder of Bedrock Manufacturing (named for the famous Flintstone's cartoon's hometown), bought the name for the company from a longtime brand of shoe polish (founded in 1907) that was best known for the slogan "You can't tell shit from Shinola." The phrase was perfection for Kartsotis, who believes that this company can someday become the largest manufacturer of high-quality watches in the United States.[1]

Kartsotis founded the company Fossil in 1984 as the United States' competitor to Swatch. During the first decade, Fossil went public in business, and the company now sells products worth over $3.2 billion that include watches, leather goods, and clothing lines. Kartsotis remained chairman of Fossil until 2010. He still owns a small part of the company.[2]

Bedrock Manufacturing started in 2003, with its Reel FX, a well-known animation studio, as one of the major players in the company's divisions. But because he felt a little unchallenged, Kartsotis thought about creating a company with a new business concept, one that he refers to as "skill at scale." With the idea of hiring and training employees to produce high-quality products made to last a lifetime, he wanted to reinvent a "heritage brand" with a compelling brand/story and make it all in America.

The company wishes to target the same consumers who were buying organic products and shopping at places that were all about being socially responsible and the customer who wishes to support local communities and keep America a thriving economy globally. Shinola hopes to be the brand reaching out to consumers who care where manufacturing takes place and who is making the product for them.[3]

The company believed there were no suitable makers of quartz analog watches in America, so it decided to partner with Ronda, a Swiss movement manufacturer, to set up its 60,000-square-foot watch factory. The new watch company's base was the famous Detroit Art Deco Argonaut Building, once the home of General Motors' research labs. Ronda supplied the components of each watch, and Detroit workers assembled each one of them with care. Producing over 500,000 watches, the company imported watch cases and dials from China because it could not source them in the United States. Shinola has been very successful in the production of watches, leading in the moderately priced category.

Each watch's final production is completed in the Argonaut factory, where leather straps are added or final parts assembled

Figure 10.1 Employee assembling Shinola watch straps. (Courtesy of Shinola)

(Figure 10.1). This last touch of the product allows Shinola to claim that its products are from the United States.[4] The company has now added a leather factory that produces watch straps, allowing customers to interchange their watch bands' colors.

Whereas most luxury Swiss watch companies have a markup of about tenfold because they use celebrity endorsement and take out substantial advertising budgets to push their watches, Shinola uses a different tactic. The company marks up its timepieces fourfold and features its employees in the ads to demonstrate the product's integrity. This approach engages consumers who like knowing who makes their watches and that they are treated with dignity and respect in the workplace. Shinola has sold thousands of timepieces through its website and in flagship stores in Detroit and New York's Tribeca (Figure 10.2).

The company now has stores across the United States in such major cities as Washington, D.C., King of Prussia, Dallas, Chicago, Plano, Minneapolis, Los Angeles, and London. Product distribution includes 350 points of sale internationally, with Shinola retails at Colette (France), Robinsons (Singapore), Palacio de Hierro (Mexico City), and Holt Renfrew (Canada). The brand is sold via various jewelers such as Jared and high-market retailers such as Neiman Marcus, Nordstrom, Bloomingdale's,

Figure 10.2 Shinola's New York Tribeca store. (Courtesy of Shinola)

Selfridges, and Saks Fifth Avenue.[5] Its online shop, Shinola.com, launched in March 2013, and in October 2014, the company expanded to the European market. The company has also opened Shinola Outlet stores that sell off all discontinued models and those products that do not sell at retail.

The Product Line and Education

Shinola built its watch and leather factories within the College for Creative Studies (CCS). It has a partnership with CCS and believes that collaboration with the college is meaningful, involving and immersing individuals in quality fashion accessory design. Students get the chance to design watches and work with the company creating prototype designs. This partnership is a true testament to the company's belief in education, not only for the community of Detroit but also for the future workers of this country. Students are not the only individuals who work for Shinola; the company also supports full-time workers in the city of Detroit (Figure 10.3).

The company's commitment to quality products is as follows:

> We believe we should never make a product if it does not last. We
> utilize handmade production processes for our watches, bicycles, leather

Figure 10.3 Shinola employees assembling watches in Detroit. (Courtesy of Shinola)

goods, and journals because these methods yield an unmatched level of quality and an unsurpassed ability to conduct quality control. We source the best possible components for all our products and work with a community of independent American manufacturers who share our commitment to using materials of an enduring nature. We individually number each of the things we make because each is special, and all are held to the same high standard. This is the expectation we have set for ourselves so that you can expect it from us. Every Shinola watch is guaranteed for life under the Shinola Guarantee, a limited lifetime warranty.[6]

This brand isn't all about watches. It sells bags, bicycles, leather goods, jewelry, journals, pens, and pet accessories. The Shinola product line is priced very reasonably for the quality (Figures 10.4 and 10.5). All these products are sold online and in the Shinola stores. This company has also impacted other American companies because it uses local US companies to help make its products. The following few sections discuss the developments of Shinola and its affiliates to demonstrate how one company is helping to keep others in the business.

Figure 10.4 and 10.5 Images of the Shinola Store in King of Prussia Mall, Pennsylvania, United States in 2019 displaying a sample of the company's assortment. (Courtesy of the author)

Watches

The first line of Shinola watches was released in March 2013. The company did a limited edition of 2,500 of their Runwell watch, which came in both a 47 mm and 40 mm size. Both timepieces sold out in two weeks, with over a third of these sales from Detroit-area residents.[7] In October of that same year, Shinola released the Wright Brothers Limited Edition watch, the first watch in its Great Americans Series, followed by the Henry Ford Pocket Watch in 2014. With the Wright Brothers Limited Edition timepiece, the company also released a bicycle. With a purchase of Shinola's limited edition watches, each person is enrolled in "The Foundry," the brand's collectors' club. I was enrolled when I purchased my Henry Ford Pocket Watch. With my membership, I received a unique welcoming postcard and a lovely series of collector postcards of images taken by the photographer Bruce Weber (who has done the famous ads for Ralph Lauren, Calvin Klein, and Abercrombie & Fitch).

In September 2014, the company collaborated with the fashion designer Oscar de la Renta and released its Latice watch. The company did a limited edition of 250 watches, with each timepiece coming with a hardcover book created exclusively for the project. The book featured an in-depth look at Oscar de la Renta and his fashion collections.[8] In 2014, Shinola released the Henry Ford Pocket Watch and the Black Buzzard titanium wristwatch as part of its Signature series. In 2015, the company's fashion assortment grew, including a Moonphase and GMT Rambler for both men and women.

While the product assortment of Shinola watches is significant (Figure 10.6), the company features various silhouettes and styles such as The Runwell: its flagship wristwatch, a timeless classic for dress, casual, and sports; The Runwell Sport: more for an active lifestyle and featuring premium parts such as a turning top-ring bezel; The Birdy: a classic tomboy style that is given feminine flavor with its double-wrap strap; The Gomelsky: a sophisticated look with a modern edge, a vintage-inspired watch that comes in a classic bracelet or double-wrap leather strap. The Detrola is a new fashion line for Shinola that gives consumers fun, hip looks at a reasonable price. Other historical silhouettes include Bedrock, Brakeman, Cass, Derby, Duck, Gail, Guardian, Muldowney, Omaha, Pee-Wee, Rambler, Sea Creatures, The Canfield, The Vinton, and the introduction of their automatic Runwell watch in 2017 after years of customers' requests. With each day, the list continues to grow, with quality as Shinola's main priority.[9]

Figure 10.6 The product assortment and line plan of Shinola watches. (Courtesy of Shinola)

Paper Journals: Edwards Brothers Malloy, Michigan

Shinola's journals and books are by Edwards Brothers Malloy, another Michigan-based company founded in 1893 and known for its quality paper products. It begins with the best raw materials from sustainably maintained American forests. While the company has evolved its production techniques over the years and uses state-of-the-art machinery, it still utilizes skilled craftspeople who are the best at making a quality product; this company leaves no stone unturned.

Bicycles: Waterford Precision Cycles, Wisconsin

The Waterford Precision Cycle factory in Wisconsin is the center for Shinola bicycles. Using lightweight, double butted chromoly steel, an expert individually handcrafts the frames and forks for each bike; the job requires careful handwork by skilled craftspeople. The products are finished at the Detroit workshop, where the rest of the bicycle pieces, including Shimano internal hubs and Shinola leather saddles are added. Master production mechanics hand-lift and custom-assemble each bike to ensure a product of impeccable quality without flaws.

Shinola Jewelry, Leather Goods, and Pet Accessories

Shinola Pet is an assortment of dog collars, beds, and toys all done in collaboration with Bruce Weber. The Shinola product line for pets supports the Michigan Humane Society and the Best Friends Animal Society in their mission to raise awareness about dog rescue. Some dog toys collaborate with Empowerment Plan, a Detroit charity that employs women living in shelters, training them to manufacture sleeping bag coats for the homeless.[10]

Sustainable Design and Branding: Interview with Chris Baeza

Chris Baeza has had an extensive twenty-plus year career as an accomplished design and merchandising executive with proven results working with iconic global brands. Chris has a strong background in fashion and has multi-tier capabilities in men's, women's, and children's fashion, and in accessories, emphasizing brand-building for different channels of distribution. Her positions in the industry have allowed her to travel worldwide, working with top companies such as Tommy Hilfiger, Hugo Boss, Adidas, Nordstrom, Dockers, and Nautica.

Her branding, textiles, design, product development, and merchandising background bring real-world experience to the classroom. Chris is a dynamic educator who provides opportunities to expand students' learning with experiential and inter-disciplinary course work and international study tours. She has a passion for ethical fashion and "for-benefit" business models. These inform her teaching philosophy where Chris strives to spark engagement for learning and developing one's character, and demonstrating the importance of relationships and collaboration. She ignites a sense of meaning and purpose and creates a classroom environment that fosters a strong work ethic.

Her research seeks to explore and answer the following overarching question: are students who study design and merchandising better prepared after graduation when ethics and social entrepreneurship are an integral part of their curricula?

Outside of the classroom, she serves as an advisor to several companies in the industry. She is a board member for Learning to Lead/Girls Take Charge and teaches workshops to high-school students who are thinking about studying fashion design or merchandising.

She holds a B.S. degree in Fashion Design and Textile Design from the Philadelphia College of Textiles & Science (Philadelphia University + Thomas Jefferson) and an M.S. degree in Leadership Development from Pennsylvania State University.

Tell us why sustainable fashion brands are so important today.

Sustainable brands are part of a renaissance happening in the textile/fashion industry. They are challenging an industry that has done and is doing damage to the planet and people working in the supply chain. Sustainable brands are raising the bar for other brands who solely put profits at the center of all decisions. What used to be "trendy" is now a moral imperative for the entire textile and fashion industry.

What are some of your favorite sustainable brands and why?

There are so many, but here are a few: Allbirds is a favorite since their mantra is "to create better things in a better way." A friend in the sneaker industry told me that about 60 percent of a sneaker's environmental impact is the material selection. The brand commits "to be like a tree, leaving the environment cleaner than we found it … we believe in the power of natural materials, and their potential to transform ecosystems." This brand has done a great job adhering to its brand ethos and creating an outstanding product that looks and feels great and is at a great price point. Know Supply is another brand whose ethos is about having the customer know who made their clothes. They produce excellent quality apparel which is ethically made and signed by the maker. Eileen Fisher is a pioneering brand who is one of the oldest brands leading the sustainable movement and continues to be an example of how brands can create beautiful products and reduce the waste the industry produces. Eileen Fisher is in many ways ahead of most brands, from a commitment to material selection and a mono-material strategy to upcycling and keeping products in use and out of landfills.

How can we become sustainable consumers of fashion?

Care about where products come from, care about the environmental impacts, and care about the people who labor to make the products we adorn ourselves with and wear. Because I believe, if you care, you will want to know the story behind products/brand. Also, consumers have a lot of power to transform the fashion system by voting with their dollars and shopping smarter versus mindlessly.

What tips would you give to someone who wants to start a sustainable fashion brand?

Get clear about your brand's ethos and what you care about doing. Ask yourself, "what are we trying to do as a company/brand?" The industry issues are complex, from the environmental impact to the social effects, and don't try to do it all. You simply won't be able to do it.

Shinola Controversy

When Detroit journalist Jon Moy drew attention to Shinola's "opportunistic marketing" and its use of nostalgia to gain profit there were mixed reactions from the public. On one side, the company claimed that it was bringing back Detroit manufacturing, but on the other side, many people felt that its "Where America is Made" slogan was somewhat misleading.[11] On June 2016, the United States Federal Trade Commission ordered the company to stop using this slogan because 100 percent of the materials used to manufacture Shinola watches are imported.[12]

New York Times reporter Alex Williams condemned the brand's use of the word "Detroit" as a marketing ploy. However, in an interview, he gives credits to the company for its job creation and support for job growth.[13] Other reporters and critics have asked, how can you hate a company that is creating jobs and giving some stability to the US market, even if you don't think their products are worth the price, and is that not retail in general? And to its credit, the company invests in employee development by offering training from watchmakers from Switzerland to build a quality product.

"Bougie Crap" and Diversification

With all retail comes development, and the irony of Shinola being a moderately priced retailer founded on the grounds of the Detroit auto industry's fall will indefinitely cause problems and inner turmoil for some customers. All cities go through change, and evolutions where once historically glamourous neighborhoods are now run down or the *wrong part of town* are not unusual. Shinola's efforts to revitalize the Cass Corridor of Detroit fell under scrutiny, but the brand successfully partnered with such retailers as Third Man Records to bring the neighborhood back to life.

Under the critical eye of the media, Shinola's Tom Kartsotis wanted the retail space to resonate with economic growth, while others thought it was just cultural fabrication and gentrification. Cynical Professor Rebekah Modrak called the opening of Shinola's store nothing but "bougie crap" and that the company "uses the design aesthetic of 'calculated authenticity' and the elements of handcraft or personalization to suggest that the product is motivated by these values and not by crass economic gain."[14]

Modrak's claims are similar to any cultural consumer theorist who believes that retailers do nothing but manipulate consumers to purchase their products. The failure behind this argument is that without customers buying the product, the business fails. And those who are employed there lose their jobs. No sales, no workforce. There is trouble with the idea that shoppers are just drones of retail capitalists. And I believe Professor Modrak misses a vital component of the argument. *We know* of manipulations, but what is important is the brand/story and the message behind those companies where we make purchases. Just go to Instagram, Facebook, or any social media, and you can see manipulation, but your own consumer choices have initiated those that pop up on your Instagram; they relate to you as a person. And to be honest, this author believes the message that Shinola delivers is much better than many of its competitors. The brand/story behind Shinola is customer education as the brand tells the story of the product using historical fact and narrative.

Additionally, the brand has given philanthropically to Detroit in more than just watch manufacturing, supporting programs such as the York Project, a streetwear company on a mission to help the homeless. Founded by Josh York, a native of Detroit, the York Project has given to over 24,000 charities across the United States. And with Shinola partnering with the York brand to develop its black and gray "Shinola" logo sweatshirts sold in its stores and online, Shinola is promoting the York Project's mission. This is genius as it allows Shinola (in this case the larger of the two companies) to share a new vendor space and thus becomes a gateway to helping the York Project's brand. The idea of Shinola as a gateway to sharing other brands with the larger public through promotions has been lost on some, but not this author. With this Shinola collaboration, both companies win and so do their employees. Sometimes you need a larger brand to help smaller ones stay afloat or even become known to new consumers. Shinola does this, showing the public new vendors that are start-ups themselves, and this type of brand goodwill is lost on some consumer critics who just see it as another ploy. But let's not forget that both York Project and Shinola are hiring the Detroit workforce and in that way are supporting the community.[15] Rebuilding a community can be seen as both good and bad, but in most cases does allow for new invention of older historical spaces and places in landmark cities like Detroit.

Spanning over five historical buildings, Shinola demonstrates historicism with the company's newest development, the Shinola Hotel. This diversification of brand/story allows customers to visit the historical Singer Building and the adjacent T.B. Rayl Co. Store known as Rayl's (a sporting goods store), plus others past retailers such as Liggett's Drug Store, Lloyd's Furs, Sally Frocks, and the Meyer Treasure Chest of Jewels. The building was established in 1915; Wirt Rowland was the architect, who would later design some of Detroit's most recognizable buildings. The hotel building has a red-brick façade with an understated limestone-clad neoclassical exterior and is adjacent to what used to be the Singer Sewing Machine Company in 1936.

With the Shinola company's new restoration there is also a new shopping mall called Parker's Alley, which includes such stores as Drought, Good Neighbor, Madcap, Madewell, Flowers for Dreams, TLB, Three Thirteen, Detroit is the New Black, Le Labo, and of course Shinola. Visiting the Shinola Hotel is the company's own version of Disney World and immerses the consumer into the brand, with each room inspired as an homage to the founding product of this retail company: the watch.[16]

As Shinola continues to grow, it reflects the true heritage of American manufacturing, employing a diverse array of workers (Figure 10.7). It maintains its mission to educate employees in the skill of making quality products that last a lifetime. In a fast-fashion world, Shinola demonstrates that there is a market of individuals who are willing to pay a little more to support US manufacturing ideology.

Figure 10.7 The employees of the Shinola Company. (Courtesy of Shinola)

Discussion Questions

1. How did Shinola fit a niche market in watchmaking? Where do the parts for its watches come from, and how does this impact our global economy?
2. How does Shinola's company structure teach and educate employees? Can you think of other companies that follow this same model?
3. Name some companies that Shinola impacts. How is it important to the overall US economy?
4. Can you think of another company (like Shinola) that markets to our humanity? What does it make? How is it the same, or how is it different?

Expand Your Knowledge

Shinola is impacting other companies such as Waterford Precision Cycles, The York Project and Edwards Brothers Malloy. Look up these brands and share with your colleagues the history of these brands. What is their brand/story? Write up your findings as a case study.

Further Exploration

Watch:
PBS News Hour, *How Shinola Turned Detroit Into a Luxury Brand* (2016), https://www.youtube.com/watch?v=zF5G9RdOG9w (accessed April 25, 2021).

Notes

Chapter 1

1   Alexandra Mondalek, "Nostalgia, Movie Stars, and Drag Queens: Inside the Coach Brand Turnaround," *Business of Fashion*, March 23, 2021https://www.businessoffashion.com/articles/marketing-pr/nostalgia-movie-stars-and-drag-queens-inside-the-coach-brand-turnaround (accessed December 17, 2021).
2   Youn-Kyoung Kim, Pauline Sullivan, and Judith Cardona Forney, *Experiential Retailing: Concepts and Strategies That Sell* (New York: Fairchild Publications, 2007), 406.
3   Evelyn Brannon, *Fashion Forecasting: Research, Analysis and Presentation*, 2nd ed. (New York: Fairchild Publications, 2005), 406.
4   Klaus Fog, Christian Budtz, and Baris Yakaboylu, *Storytelling: Branding in Practice* (Copenhagen: Springer 2005), 13–25.
5   Ibid., 23.
6   Ibid., 31.
7   Adam Adamson, *Brandsimple: How the Best Brands Keep It Simple and Succeed* (New York: Palgrave Macmillan, 2006), 181–3.

Chapter 2

1   Charles W. King, "A Rebuttal to the 'Trickle Down' Theory," in *Towards Scientific Marketing*, ed. Stephen A. Greyer (Chicago, IL: American Marketing Association, 1963), 108–25.
2   Youn-Kyoung Kim, Pauline Sullivan, and Judith Cardona Forney, *Experiential Retailing: Concepts and Strategies That Sell* (New York: Fairchild Publications, 2007), 26–7.
3   Patricia Cunningham, "From Underwear to Swimwear Branding at Atlas and B.V.D. in the 1930s," *Journal of American Culture* 31, no. 1 (2009): 38–52.
4   Roland Barthes, *The Fashion System* (New York: Columbia University Press, 1985), 3–18.
5   Stuart Hall, "Encoding and Decoding in the Television Discourse," University of Birmingham, 1973, https://www.birmingham.ac.uk/Documents/college-artslaw/history/cccs/stencilled-occasional-papers/1to8and11to24and38to48/SOP07.pdf (accessed April 11, 2021).

6   Ibid.
7   Jean Baudrillard, "The System of Objects," in *Jean Baudrillard: Selected Writings*, ed. Mark Poster (Stanford, CA: Stanford University Press, 1988), 19.
8   Ibid., 170.
9   Ibid., 17.
10 Ibid., 19.
11 Asa Berger, *The Portable Postmodernist* (Walnut Creek, CA: Altamira Press, 2003), 87.
12 Ibid.
13 Ibid., 79.
14 Ibid., 87.
15 Marcia A. Morgado, "Fashion Phenomena and the Post-Postmodern Condition: Enquiry and Speculation," *Fashion, Style & Popular Culture* 1, no. 3 (2014): 313–39.
16 Marcia A. Morgado, personal communication with author, February 2, 2019.
17 Morgado, "Fashion Phenomena and the Post-Postmodern Condition," 319.
18 Gwendolyn O'Neal, "Fashioning Future Fashion," in *Fashioning the Future: Our Future from Our Past*, ed. Patricia Cunningham and Gayle Strege (Columbus, OH: Ohio State Historic Costume & Textiles Collection, 1996), 27.
19 Ibid.
20 Ibid., 28.
21 Judith Williamson, *Decoding Advertisements: Ideology and Meaning in Advertising* (New York: Marion Boyars Publishing, 2002), 12.
22 Jean A. Hamilton, "The Macro-Micro Interface in the Construction of Individual Fashion Forms and Meaning," *Clothing and Textiles Research Journal* 15, no. 3 (1997): 165–71.
23 Ibid., 165.
24 Ibid., 167.
25 Matthew Debord, "Texture and Taboo: The Tyranny of Texture and Ease in the J.Crew Catalog," *Fashion Theory* 1, no. 3 (1997): 261–78.
26 Ibid., 263.
27 Douglas Holt, *How Brands Become Icons* (Boston, MA: Harvard Business School Press, 2004), 215.
28 Ibid., 209.
29 Ibid., 210.
30 Ibid., 211.
31 Laurence Vincent, *Legendary Brands: Unleashing the Power of Storytelling to Create Winning Market Strategy* (Chicago, IL: Dearborn Trading Publishing, 2002), 25.
32 Ibid.
33 Ibid., 123.
34 Ibid.
35 Ibid., 127.
36 Teri Agins, *The End of Fashion* (New York: William Morrow, 1999), 14–15.
37 Marc Gobé, *Emotional Branding: The New Paradigm for Connecting Brands to People* (New York: Allworth Press, 2001), xvii.

38 Grant McCracken, *Culture and Consumption* (Bloomington, IN: Indiana University Press, 1988), 71–89.
39 Grant McCracken, *Culture and Consumption II* (Bloomington, IN: Indiana University Press, 2005), 162–70.
40 Ibid., 177.
41 Ibid., 178–91.
42 Sarah Davis and Lauren Toney, "How Coronavirus (COVID-19) Is Impacting Ecommerce [March 2021]," *ROI Revolution*, https://www.roirevolution.com/blog/2021/03/coronavirus-and-ecommerce/ (accessed April 11, 2021).
43 Sandra L. Colby and Jennifer M. Ortman, "Projections of the Size and Composition of the U.S. Population: 2014 to 2060," *U.S. Census Bureau*, http://www.census.gov/content/dam/Census/library/publications/2015/demo/p25-1143.pdf (accessed 11 April 2021).
44 *Auntie Mame*, Dir. Morton DaCosta, Warner Brothers, United States, December 1958.

Chapter 3

1   Teri Agins, *The End of Fashion* (New York: William Morrow, 1999), 14–15.
2   Ralph Lauren, *Ralph Lauren* (New York: Rizzoli, 2007).
3   Michael Gross, *Genuine Authentic: The Real Life of Ralph Lauren* (New York: Perennial, 2003).
4   Colin McDowell, *Ralph Lauren: The Man, the Vision, the Style* (New York: Rizzoli, 2003).
5   Ibid., 15.
6   Gross, *Genuine Authentic*, xvii.
7   McDowell, *Ralph Lauren*, 20.
8   Buffy Birrittella, "The Big Knot," *Daily News Record*, December 19, 1967.
9   McDowell, *Ralph Lauren*, 29.
10 Lauren, *Ralph Lauren*, 399.
11 Ibid.
12 McDowell, *Ralph Lauren*, 202.
13 Ibid.
14 Gross, *Genuine Authentic*, 170.
15 McDowell, *Ralph Lauren*, 202.
16 Lauren, *Ralph Lauren*, 410.
17 McDowell, *Ralph Lauren*, 202.
18 Ibid.
19 Ibid., 417–18.
20 Ibid., 434.
21 Ibid., 417–18.
22 Ibid., 434.
23 Ibid., 437.
24 Ibid.
25 Ibid., 203.

26 Raquel Laneri and Connie Wang, "Ralph Lauren Runs an Assimilation-Themed Campaign," *Refinery 29*, https://www.refinery29.com/en-us/ralph-lauren-native-appropriation (accessed March 25, 2021).

27 McDowell, *Ralph Lauren*, 203.

28 Ibid.

29 See company history at https://www.ralphlauren.com/rl-50-timeline-feat (accessed February 6, 2022).

Chapter 4

1 Holly Price Alford and Anne Stegemeyer, *Who's Who in Fashion* (New York: Bloomsbury Fairchild Books, 2014), 414.

2 Ibid.

3 Ibid.

4 Deborah Orr, "When Vivienne Westwood Talks, We Should Listen," *The Gentlewoman* 9 (Spring/Summer 2014): 114–25.

5 Vivienne Westwood and Ian Kelly, *Vivienne Westwood* (London: Picador, 2015), 419.

6 Claire Wilcox, *Vivienne Westwood* (London: V&A Publications, 2004), 12.

7 Ibid., 13–14.

8 Ibid., 17.

9 Ibid., 18.

10 Ibid., 19.

11 Ibid., 210.

12 Westwood and Kelly, *Vivienne Westwood*, 422.

13 Ibid.

14 Ibid.

15 Gozde Goncu-Berk, "Fashion Trends," *Bloomsbury Fashion Central*, https://www.bloomsburyfashioncentral.com/products/berg-fashion-library/article/bibliographical-guides/fashion-trends (accessed March 24, 2021).

Chapter 5

1 Eric Wilson, "Vera Wang's Business Is No Longer All Dressed in White," *New York Times*, December 15, 2005.

2 A&E Television Networks, *Fashion: Icons of Fashion*, 2001, DVD.

3 Ibid.

4 Holly Price Alford and Anne Stegemeyer, *Who's Who in Fashion*, 6th ed. (New York: Bloomsbury, 2014), 410.

5 A&E Television Networks, *Fashion: Icons of Fashion*.

6 Associated Press, "Vera Wang to Design Line for Just Kohl's," *USA Today*, August 24, 2006.

7 Ibid.

8 Ibid.

9 Emily Lung, personal communication with author, September 15, 2007.

Chapter 6

1 Gap Inc., "Gap Inc.'s Global Footprint," *Gapinc.com* https://gapinc-prod. azureedge.net/gapmedia/gapcorporatesite/media/images/docs/global-footprint-q4-20_2_8_21.pdf (accessed April 19, 2021).
2 Gap Inc., "History," *Gapinc.com* https://www.gapinc.com/en-us/about/ history (accessed April 23, 2021).
3 Ibid.
4 Editors of GQ, "GQ for Gap 2018: The Iconic Sweatshirt, Reimagined," *GQ*, https://www.gq.com/story/gq-for-gap-2018-hoodies-reveal (accessed April 23, 2021).
5 Gap Inc., "History."
6 Lard & Partners, *Individuals* (New York: Melcher Media, 2006), 7.
7 Jean A. Hamilton, "The Macro-Micro Interface in the Construction of Individual Fashion Forms and Meaning," *Clothing and Textiles Research Journal* 15, no. 3 (1997): 165–71.
8 Gap Inc., "History."
9 Christopher Corbett, "Ever-Chic Khaki and the Profitable Fascists," *The Washington Post*, September 26, 1993, https://www.washingtonpost. com/archive/opinions/1993/09/26/ever-chic-khaki-and-the-fashionable-fascist/946ed5df-3225-44c6-813a-34a7b3f872bb/ (accessed April 23, 2021).
10 https://www.youtube.com/watch?v=E9zk4ZNnNOk (accessed April 23, 2021).
11 https://www.youtube.com/watch?v=knW1hGwmEXQ (accessed April 23, 2021).
12 https://www.youtube.com/watch?v=8989t_xRsls (accessed April 23, 2021).
13 Sharon Edelson, "Gap Readies Minimum Wage Increase," *WWD*, February 19, 2014, https://wwd.com/business-news/government-trade/gap-boosts-wages-7486344/ (accessed April 23, 2021).
14 Gap Inc., "History."
15 Matthew Stern, "Gap Plans Move into Non-Apparel Categories," *Retail Wire*, May 8, 2020, https://www.retailwire.com/discussion/gap-plans-move-into-non-apparel-categories/ (accessed April 23, 2021).
16 Kim Bhasin, "Gap Has Billion-Dollar Ambitions for Yeezy Deal with Kanye West," *Bloomberg*, March 17, 2021, https://www.bloomberg.com/news/ articles/2021-03-17/kanye-west-and-gap-have-billion-dollar-ambitions-for-yeezy-deal (accessed April 24, 2021).
17 King Sukii, "Aurora James, Melissa King & More Tapped for 'Generation Good' Gap Campaign," *Cassius Life*, February 22, 2021, https://cassiuslife. com/391051/gap-generation-good-campaign-photos/ (accessed April 24, 2021).

Chapter 7

1 Estée Lauder Companies, "Investors," https://www.elcompanies.com/en/ investors (accessed February 7, 2021).

2   Ibid.
3   Ibid.
4   Ibid.
5   Anne-Marie Schiro, "Frank Angelo, 49, Cosmetics Innovator, Dies," *New York Times*, January 17, 1997, http://www.nytimes.com/1997/01/17/us/frank-angelo-49-cosmetics-innovator-dies.html (accessed February 7, 2021).
6   Danielle Pergament, "The Ringleader: M.A.C.: How a Weird Indie Startup Took Over the World of Makeup," *Allure.com*, http://www.allure.com/beauty-trends/how-to/2013/the-history-of-mac-cosmetics (accessed February 7, 2021).
7   MAC AIDS Fund, "Campaign History," https://www.macaidsfund.org/theglam/campaignhistory (accessed February 7, 2021).
8   Ibid.
9   Jennifer Fulton and Joseph H. Hancock II, "Stephen Cal/Stephanie Chic: A Student and a Queen," *Fashion, Style & Popular Culture* 1, no. 1 (2014): 119–30.
10 MAC AIDS Fund, "Campaign History."
11 Lee Barron, "The Habitus of Elizabeth Hurley: Celebrity, Fashion, and Identity Branding," in *The Fashion Business Reader*, ed. Joseph H. Hancock II and Anne Peirson-Smith (London and New York: Bloomsbury Press, 2019), 267–77.
12 MAC Cosmetics, "Viva Glam Archives: 25 Years of Giving a Glam," https://www.maccosmetics.com/vivaglam-timeline (accessed February 10, 2021).
13 Ibid.
14 Armando Falaco, "M.A.C. Cosmetics' Gender-Neutral Makeup Popup Store in Liverpool ONE – 15th October 2019," *MintelReports* https://reports-mintel-com.ezproxy2.library.drexel.edu/display/980594/?fromSearch=%3Ffilters.category%3D25%26freetext%3DM.A.C.%2520Cosmetics%26last_filter%3Dcategory (accessed February 10, 2021)

Chapter 8

1   Levi Strauss & Co., "History & Heritage," http://www.levistrauss.com/our-story/heritage-timeline/ (accessed February 10, 2021).
2   Ibid.
3   Ibid.
4   Ibid.
5   Ibid.
6   https://www.youtube.com/watch?v=Q56M5OZS1A8 (accessed February 10, 2021).
7   Levi Strauss & Co., "History & Heritage."
8   https://www.youtube.com/watch?v=DF-mbNVkT5I (accessed February 10, 2021).
9   Levi Strauss & Co., "History & Heritage."
10 Dun & Bradstreet, Levi Strauss & Co, https://www.dnb.com/business-directory/company-profiles.levi_strauss__co.3c529f752bf03164c1edd33ddd234c4a.html (accessed January 7, 2021).

Chapter 9

1   Mahsa Shahbandeh, "U.S. Eyewear Industry – Statistics & Facts," *Statista*, October 22, 2021, https://www.statista.com/topics/1470/eyewear-in-the-us/#dossierKeyfigures (accessed January 8, 2022).

2   Ibid.

3   Emily Krol, "Eyeglasses and Contact Lenses—US—September 2013," *MintelReports*, http://academic.mintel.com.ezproxy2.library.drexel.edu/display/637753/ (accessed March 15, 2021).

4   Ibid.

5   Ibid.

6   Ibid.

/   Ibid.

8   Ibid.

9   Vanessa O'Connell, "Warby Parker Co-Founder Says Initial Vision Was All About Price," *Wall Street Journal*, July 18, 2012, http://www.wsj.com/articles/SB10000872396390444097904577535111565440718 (accessed March 15, 2021).

10 Laura Zax, "The VisionSpring Model: Creating Markets and Players Instead of Empty CSR," *Forbes.com*, October 5, 2012, http://www.forbes.com/sites/ashoka/2012/10/05/the-visionspring-model-creating-markets-and-players-instead-of-empty-csr/ (accessed May 18, 2015).

11 Krol, "Eyeglasses and Contact Lenses."

12 Michael J. De La Merced, "J.Crew Chief and American Express Invest in Warby Parker," *New York Times*, February 24, 2013, http://dealbook.nytimes.com/2013/02/24/j-crew-chief-and-american-express-invest-in-warby-parker/?_r=0 (accessed May 18, 2015).

13 Serena Saitto and Leslie Picker, "Funds Think Warby Parker Is Worth $1 Billion," *Bloomberg.com*, http://www.bloomberg.com/news/articles/2015-03-04/warby-parker-said-to-draw-fund-interest-at-over-1-billion-value (accessed March 15, 2021).

14 Warby Parker, "Culture," https://www.warbyparker.com/culture (accessed March 15, 2021).

15 www.youtube.com/watch?v=lV-afyZ46aQa (accessed March 15, 2021).

16 Dennis R. Shaughnessy, "The Public Capital Markets and Etsy and Warby Parker," *SEI at Northeastern*, https://www.northeastern.edu/sei/2018/10/the-public-capital-markets-and-etsy-and-warby-parker/ (accessed March 15, 2021).

Chapter 10

1   Schumpeter, "Making it in America: Mo' time for Motown," *Economist*, February 5, 2014, http://www.economist.com/blogs/schumpeter/2014/02/making-it-america (accessed March 22, 2021).

2   Ibid.

3   Ibid.

4   Ibid.

5 Ibid.
6 Shinola Detroit, Fact Sheet 2014, p. 2.
7 John Gallagher, "Shinola Sold Out of Limited-Edition Watches," *Detroit Free Press*, March 20, 2013, http://archive.freep.com/article/20130320/BUSINESS06/130320035/Shinola-sold-out-of-limited-edition-watches (accessed March 22, 2021).
8 Hannah Elliott, "Shinola and Oscar de la Renta: Motown and Madison Avenue Make a Watch," *Forbes.com*, June 27, 2014, http://www.forbes.com/sites/hannahelliott/2014/06/27/shinola-and-oscar-de-la-renta-motown-and-madison-avenue-make-a-watch/ (accessed March 22, 2021).
9 Shinola Detroit, WatchStraps, 2022, https://www.shinola.com/watch-straps.html (accessed January 11, 2021).
10 "Bruce Weber Partners with Shinola for New Line of Pet Accessories," *Edge MediaNetwork*, August 29, 2014, http://www.edgemedianetwork.com/style/home/features//164838/bruce_weber_partners_with_shinola_for_new_line_of_pet_accessories (accessed March 22, 2021).
11 Jon Moy, "On Shinola, Detroit's Misguided White Knight," March 26, 2014,https://www.complex.com/style/shinola-detroits-misguided-white-knight (accessed March 22, 2021).
12 Ibid.
13 Alex Williams, "Shinola Takes Its 'Detroit Cool' Message on the Road," *New York Times*, January 6, 2016, https://www.nytimes.com/2016/01/07/fashion/shinola-watches-bicycles-leather-goods-expansion.html (accessed March 22, 2021).
14 Rebekah Modrak, "Bougie Crap: Art, Design, and Gentrification," *Infinite Mile Detroit*, issue 14, February 2015,https://infinitemiledetroit.com/Bougie_Crap_Art,_Design_and_Gentrification.html (accessed March 22, 2021).
15 Shinola, "York Project: The Detroit Streetwear Company Mission to Help the Homeless," *The Journal*, October 22, 2018, https://www.shinola.com/thejournal/york-project-detroit-streetwear-company-mission-help-homeless (accessed April 23, 2021).
16 https://www.shinolahotel.com/the-history (accessed March 22, 2021).

Index